Spellcrafting and White Magic

Unlocking the Secrets of Protection Spells, Blessings, Spellcasting, Candle Magick, and Wiccan Rituals

© **Copyright 2023 - All rights reserved.**

The content contained within this book may not be reproduced, duplicated, or transmitted without direct written permission from the author or the publisher.

Under no circumstances will any blame or legal responsibility be held against the publisher, or author, for any damages, reparation, or monetary loss due to the information contained within this book, either directly or indirectly.

Legal Notice:

This book is copyright protected. It is only for personal use. You cannot amend, distribute, sell, use, quote, or paraphrase any part, or the content within this book, without the consent of the author or publisher.

Disclaimer Notice:

Please note the information contained within this document is for educational and entertainment purposes only. All effort has been executed to present accurate, up-to-date, reliable, and complete information. No warranties of any kind are declared or implied. Readers acknowledge that the author is not engaging in the rendering of legal, financial, medical, or professional advice. The content within this book has been derived from various sources. Please consult a licensed professional before attempting any techniques outlined in this book.

By reading this document, the reader agrees that under no circumstances is the author responsible for any losses, direct or indirect, that are incurred as a result of the use of the information contained within this document, including, but not limited to, errors, omissions, or inaccuracies.

Your Free Gift
(only available for a limited time)

Thanks for getting this book! If you want to learn more about various spirituality topics, then join Mari Silva's community and get a free guided meditation MP3 for awakening your third eye. This guided meditation mp3 is designed to open and strengthen ones third eye so you can experience a higher state of consciousness. Simply visit the link below the image to get started.

https://spiritualityspot.com/meditation

Or, Scan the QR code!

Table of Contents

PART 1: SPELLCRAFTING 1
    INTRODUCTION 2
    CHAPTER 1 – THE ART OF SPELLCRAFTING 4
    CHAPTER 2 – ELEMENTS AND MAGICKAL CORRESPONDENCES 11
    CHAPTER 3 – THE SPELLCRAFTER'S TOOLKIT 24
    CHAPTER 4 – GETTING STARTED WITH RITUAL 34
    CHAPTER 5 – PROTECTION AND DEFENSE SPELLS 42
    CHAPTER 6 – MAGIC HERBS AND PLANTS 51
    CHAPTER 7 – CANDLE MAGICK SPELLS 58
    CHAPTER 8 – SEASONAL SPELLS FOR SABBATS 67
    CHAPTER 9 – HEALTH, WEALTH, AND ABUNDANCE SPELLS 78
    CHAPTER 10 – LOVE SPELLS AND CHARMS 88
    CONCLUSION 95

PART 2: WHITE MAGIC 96
    INTRODUCTION 97
    CHAPTER 1: A BRIEF HISTORY OF WHITE MAGIC 99
    CHAPTER 2: GETTING STARTED WITH WICCA: A WHITE MAGIC CRAFT 110
    CHAPTER 3: PROTECTION MAGICK 101: HOW TO HANDLE THE NASTIES 119
    CHAPTER 4: CANDLE MAGICK FOR THE WHITE WITCH 128
    CHAPTER 5: MAGICAL BLESSING RITUALS TO SPREAD YOUR LIGHT 136

CHAPTER 6: THE WHITE WITCH'S APOTHECARY 144
CHAPTER 7: HEAL THYSELF...LIKE WHITE WITCHES DO 154
CHAPTER 8: CELEBRATIONS OF THE WHITE WITCH 163
CHAPTER 9: SPELLCRAFTING FOR GOOD PURPOSES 172
CHAPTER 10: WORKING WITH SPIRIT GUIDES 180
CONCLUSION 188
HERE'S ANOTHER BOOK BY MARI SILVA THAT YOU MIGHT LIKE 190
YOUR FREE GIFT (ONLY AVAILABLE FOR A LIMITED TIME) 191
RESOURCES 192

Part 1: Spellcrafting

The Ultimate Spellcraft Guide for Beginners Wanting to Create Spells and Learn Spellcasting

Introduction

Are you interested in increasing your knowledge about spellcrafting even further? As an ancient art that contributed a lot to several religions and cultures worldwide, spellcrafting is a great skill to master. It is the key to creating spells and magic that will work to your best advantage.

If you like anything related to spells and magic, this book about spellcrafting can help. With this reading material, you will have a practical, easy-to-follow, and accessible guide containing all the things you should know about crafting and casting effective spells. This means that spells, otherwise called witches' prayers, are those that everyone can learn and eventually master.

The good news is that you don't have to get involved in a mystery cult or promise to serve a god or goddess so you can start crafting spells. You don't also need to convert to or denounce a religion. All you have to do is read this book and grasp every bit of information included here.

The details included in this reading material are all easy to understand and follow. Even those concepts that are otherwise difficult to understand are simplified to ensure that readers will not have a hard time absorbing their meanings and significance. Most of the instructions about casting spells included here are also practical and easy to apply.

After reading this book, you will surely have a much clearer understanding of spells and magic. You will know how magical energy works and the secrets to spellcrafting. With that, you will be on your way towards tapping your inner power and focus, so you can guide and direct them while you use just simple items and ingredients.

Just make sure you also have an open mind, patience, will, courage, self-conviction, and genuine desire before following what's instructed in this book. With all the mentioned qualities, you can easily follow what is in your heart and be mature enough to take full responsibility for every step and action you undertake as you start crafting your own spells.

Chapter 1 – The Art of Spellcrafting

First and foremost, spellcrafting, also called spell-making, is an art in the world of magic. It is the art of crafting or creating unique spells either by making your own from scratch or by combining different spells that are already existing. If you use existing spells, you can modify or change them a bit so you can use them for your desired result.

Remember that trying to learn the art of spellcrafting requires a lot of patience, as it takes time for you to master it and put your knowledge to practical use. Customizing your spells is likely to produce more than one effect, like fire and frost damage.

The effect's magnitude will also be proportional to the specific magic needed in casting the spell. Several effects also tend to meet compounding magic requirements.

Spell Defined

In its basic form, a spell refers to your intent to enforce a change using energy. You can manifest it in various ways. It could be through dancing and chanting or elaborate rituals that require the participation of many people for a few days,

There are instances when rituals are only spiritual, practiced mainly to honor a deity or celebrate an important holiday. The rituals, therefore, do not necessarily require the presence of spells. Also, note that sometimes, spells have physical ingredients. At the same time, in other instances, they need nothing else except for the energy you are raising. However, every spell has similar basic components regardless of how elaborate it is.

One more fact about spells is that even if they are common, you can't perceive them immediately as inherently religious. They do not also necessarily form part of just a single practice. As a matter of fact, contrary to what a lot of people believe, the majority of religions worldwide use spells - among which are Christians. Take the act of prayer as an example.

Every time you pray, you tend to set an intent, raise your energy, then release it to the universe. The process may also involve summoning a sort of deity so you can receive aid in manifesting your prayer. In most cases, you can expect the deity to perform almost all the legwork for you, which lessens the activity on your part. With that, it is no longer surprising to see prayer being easily distinguishable compared to other active types and forms of spellwork.

The act of crafting and casting spells is not also just contemporary; spells have existed since prehistoric times, making it a truly ancient magical practice. Aside from that, remember that while you can look at prayer as a religious act, the use of spells is usually secular.

This means that anyone can access spells regardless of what religion they believe in. With that, it is no longer surprising to find witches who practice the art of spellcrafting and witchcraft while strongly believing in Jesus and God.

The Art of Spellcrafting and Witchcraft for Beginners

As mentioned just a while ago, spellcrafting is an art that requires a lot of time, patience, and commitment to master. Contrary to what many believe, learning witchcraft, magic, and the art of crafting spells is not easy. It is not a quick way to gain your desired results and rewards. It is more than just following instructions, like lighting a candle and saying some words; there is so much more involved in the process.

For instance, you can view spells as art resembling recipes. The reason is that they allow you to follow along. However, suppose you are unfamiliar with the ingredients and the techniques. In that case, the entire process will likely be a hit or miss. As you depend more on the recipe without comprehending the things that compose them and what makes them work, it is also highly probable that you will experience more misses instead of hits.

The same premise is applicable in witchcraft and spellcrafting. Like any other skill, it involves more than just following recipe instructions. You have to understand every component and element of it to judge if it is good enough or has flaws. In other words, the whole process is more than just sticking to spells written by other people.

Merely trusting it is not enough. It is not also enough to adhere to and follow the instructions and hope that the best outcome comes from it. It requires learning everything about the spell. You have to be familiar with the components (ingredients) and the techniques and tools used in the process.

Spellcrafting and spellcasting are, therefore, not as easy as writing some words and expressing them aloud as you wave a wand or piece of wood while anticipating that it will produce your desired results. It involves a lot of work, including the gathering of information and spell ingredients. Some deep reflection is also necessary. You should think of what you do and why.

For instance, you need to think of and reflect on what you ask or expect a certain gemstone or herb to do for you. By doing that, you will be able to make your mind focus or concentrate. Also, you have to ensure that every word in your spell is concise and well thought out. This should not leave any room for misinterpretation or confusion.

The Language of Magic

When it comes to spellcrafting, make it a point to truly understand the language of magic. Note that words are not only elements of writing or speech, as they are also powerful enough that you can use them to strengthen the effects of a spell or magic. Speaking the words aloud can even transform them into vibrations and frequencies.

You can use the right vibrations and frequencies to control and direct energy. Since the vibrations and frequencies of words hold power designed to keep energy under control, learning and understanding how you can use the correct magic words should be the first thing you should do in spellcrafting and creating magic effects.

Also, remember that the words you will use in magic can be expressed in various forms. You can say them in the form of not only spells but also prayers, incantations, and songs. The reason why they are in various forms is that words have a great impact on the world we are presently living in.

Words spoken with a sound are also useful in directing energy – the kind of energy that can produce magical effects. Once you know how to do that, you will realize that words hold the same power as swords.

Traditional Words Used in Magic and Spells

As you may have already known by now, words play a major role in the world of making and crafting spells. The language you use in your spells can have a say on how effective they will be. Some of the most commonly used traditional and empowered words in the world of magic are the following:

Abracadabra

This seemingly nonsense word that has already been passed on several generations is very impressive. Originally, the word *abracadabra* was already considered magic. Ever since, many magicians, witches, spell makers, and casters have used the word *abracadabra* as a form of charm that gives them protection against every kind of evil, as well as illness and bad luck.

At that time, the word was supposedly written on one piece of papyrus several times. The last letter of the word has to be dropped on every line until the one who practiced magic successfully reduced the word into just one letter, specifically the letter "a," which is the last one.

Once the word abracadabra reached the English during the 16th century, many no longer used it as a physical charm. It turned into an incantation designed to offer protection from evil. After several centuries, the abracadabra word started to lose a lot of its mystical potency. Upon reaching the 19th century, abracadabra turned into a word you can connect with conjurers.

Hocus Pocus

There is also the word *hocus pocus*, which you can associate with the process of executing some transformation or trick. This word also underwent a bit of tricky and challenging transformation.

When the word "hocus pocus" came to English during the early 1600s, it was specifically used to describe jugglers. When the 1600 century was coming to an end, the word hocus-pocus started to be used to refer to the cry of a conjurer, the sleight of hand, or as a reference to a form of nonsense or trickery.

Open Sesame

Who has not heard of the word "open sesame"? A famous line in the movies, open sesame is also ideal for use in the world of magic and spellcrafting. Before the 1600s, this line became a famous opening spell that provided wizards passage even in locked doors. This happens by ripping the doors from the hinges and then letting them get torn to the firewood. You can also use this powerful word in modern spells, especially if you intend to open up something positive, like certain opportunities.

Modern-day Spellcrafting

When it comes to modern-day spellcrafting, strengthening your mind is a necessity. The reason is that the most vital tool when it comes to creating spells is no longer the candle, the cauldron, or the spell book; it is your mind. Developing a stronger mind means you will also improve at creating spells. You need a strong mental aptitude in modern-day spellcrafting so you can do the following:

- Retain your focus for a prolonged period
- Move willingly from one phase of consciousness to another
- Improve your sensory abilities and perceptions
- Gain access to the untapped components of your subconscious and conscious minds with ease
- Manipulate or control your energy – You raise, hold, release, or direct it.

Strengthening your mind works similarly to when you are strengthening your other muscles. You can also do a few psychic exercises designed to boost your mental abilities. Aside from that, you can try meditation, as it is a great way to train your mind to become even stronger.

A lot of traditional tools for Wicca have a strong association with witchcraft. Several of these tools were the ones inherited from ceremonial magic. The good thing about them is that they tend to work well. It is the reason why people, regardless of their paths, make use of them.

Modern witchcraft and spellcrafting, therefore, give practitioners, often the average people, the freedom to work on anything based on their own preferences rather than using traditional tools. As an important tip, you must learn and understand the tools you intend to use. Try experimenting with them and determining the specific ones that suit your personality and needs the most.

In modern spellcrafting, there is no need to get a cauldron or any other traditional tool if you feel like it is unnecessary. Some find it an indispensable part of the process of creating and casting spells. Still, if you feel you don't need one, you can use other tools that fit your preference and personal style.

Also, contrary to what the media depicts, witchcraft can be just a basic art. It is not exclusively meant for evil purposes, unlike what the media in the form of movies and other forms of entertainment demonstrate. As a matter of fact, you can use spells to attract everything that is good and positive or to ward off evil and negative energy from your home and life.

If your mind is extremely well-disciplined, you can practice this magic form without any tools. Still, most modern practitioners feel like they should use some tools designed to improve their focus and symbolize whatever it is they want from the spells. They also use these tools in drawing, borrowing, and manipulating energies.

In the beginning, there is a high chance that you will greatly depend on certain tools when crafting and making spells. Once you master everything, you can drop such reliance on the tools, especially once you notice your mind becoming stronger. You can start relying on the power of your mind to make spells that work.

The Wiccan Rede

When it comes to the ethical practice of crafting and casting spells, the Wiccan Rede tends to play a very vital role. Before you complete any spell or ritual, you need to fully understand the Wiccan Rede, which only consists of eight powerful words that remind practitioners to never do any harm.

"An Ye Harm None, Do What Ye Will"

The Wiccan rede has a full version, which is longer, but it revolves around that 8-word code of conduct. By taking to heart what the Wiccan rede states, you will be fully guided in practicing the art of spellcrafting. You will know exactly how you should act and perform magickal work while ensuring that you also take responsibility for every action you take. It serves as your way to practice magick ethically.

The same guideline or rule is what you can find in Aleister Crowley's works wherein he offered advice to his readers through this line, *"Do what thou wilt shall be the whole of the law. Love is the law, love under will".*

Crowley coined the term "magick," which means that it is an actual term, not a typo or a misspelling. Magick was mostly used by Thelemic and ceremonial practitioners. Crowley coined this term to differentiate and show the occult associated with performing magic.

Magick practitioners also define it as a science and art aiming to stimulate change while confirming with the will. It even encompasses mundane acts of will and ritual magic.

Crowley also perceived magick as a vital technique for anyone who intends to gain a real understanding of themselves and act based on their true will. It, therefore, serves as a way to reconcile free will and destiny. In his writings, he explained that, theoretically, it is possible to trigger a change in any object that is naturally capable of doing that.

As far as the Wiccan Rede, and all its other versions, including that of Crowley, are concerned, they mainly serve as a simple guideline. Note that you can't find universal ethical standards and rules for modern pagans and magic practitioners. With that, it is unreasonable to assume that all pagans will adhere to the Wiccan Rede.

Still, it would be much better for you to stick to the Wiccan rede of not doing any harm whenever you craft and cast spells. If you want to practice spellcrafting, you have to constantly remind yourself of your good intention.

Combined with your thoughtful action, your intention will come to life while ensuring that you practice the art of making and casting spells based on ethics. This means that even if you are performing a sort of magic, you still treat everyone with respect and fairness.

By performing magic and creating spells based on ethics and what is right, you will surely be able to make the most out of it, allowing yourself to bask in the power of being one with the energies and rhythms of the earth.

Chapter 2 – Elements and Magickal Correspondences

Correspondences are among the most vital parts of crafting and casting spells. You have to consider these correspondences every time you practice the art of spellcrafting. Note that colors, scents, and symbols are primary components of all forms of spells as they are capable of stimulating your senses while setting your overall tone.

In the world of magic, correspondences serve as representations of the relationship between natural and magical realities or between physical and psychic realities. It is not a new concept and idea, really, but the first time relational terminology was established was during the 18th century. It was coined by Emanuel Swedenborg, a theologian during that time, in his works, including Heaven and Hella and the Arcana Coelestia.

Swedenborg's proposal legitimized the notions and philosophies of correspondences that were already long-held between things, like speech and thought, action and intention, body and mind, and physical and psychic planes. The correspondences recognized between one's physical and psychic planes of operation and existence extend to every object found in the physical world.

For instance, you can expect the light to have a strong correspondence to wisdom, considering that wisdom can enlighten your mind. In contrast, light works to enlighten the eye. The same principle can be applied to warmth. Warmth strongly corresponds to love since love can warm the mind in such a way that heat warms the body.

With the proven importance of magical correspondences, it is no longer surprising to see a table listing all concepts, objects, and beings perceived to have a strong connection to supernatural beings. You can find these correspondence tables in many modern books that talk about the occult and magic. You can use them as reference tools in crafting and casting them. We will tackle some of the correspondences that you can find in such tables here.

Elemental Correspondences

The elemental correspondences encompass fire, water, air, and earth. They serve as the classical elements of magic that also have the fifth in the form of spirit, quintessence, or aether, which serves as the binding force. One important fact about these elements/elemental correspondences is that they embody the realms of the cosmos, which is where you can expect things to exist.

The classic thinking of the Greeks made them categorize the elemental correspondences based on water content and temperature. For instance, the air is mainly moist and secondarily warm. Then there is fire, which is mainly warm and secondarily dry; water, which is mainly cool, then secondarily moist; and earth, which is mainly dry and cool secondarily.

Modern-day paganism also puts a lot of focus and emphasis on the mentioned four elements. Each element has a strong connection to meanings and traits and the compass directions.

Also, note that in the world of magick, the different elements here serve as determinants. You can see these elements represented on the pentagram, with each one having various properties playing vital roles in the workings and preparations of rituals.

The elements symbolize the states, polarities, elevation levels, and directions, among many others. These elemental correspondences are also vital as they comprise two polarities – one of which is active while the other is passive. Remember that the universe has no such thing as bad or good. The reason is that specific laws and principles govern everything.

Moreover, in terms of preparing rituals, the Supreme power will be the one who will choose the specific number of elements you can use. That said, expect some rituals to need just one element while others need at least two elements.

To give you an even better idea about the elemental correspondences, here are the elements and their representations.

Earth

The earth element strongly represents stability, wisdom, security, strength, permanence, abundance, wealth, materialism, patience, responsibility, truth, prosperity, and practicality. Some of the symbols used when referring to the earth are rocks, mountains, soil, trees, and the earth itself. The earth is also recognized as the most dependable and stable of all the elements. It can sustain life and is known for being so stable that other elements also rely on it.

- **Direction** - North
- **Color** - Yellow
- **Qualities** - heavy and passive, cold and dry
- **Metal** - Mercury, lead
- **Zodiac signs** - Virgo, Capricorn, Taurus
- **Types of magic** - Tree magic, fertility magic, rune casting, prosperity, herbal lore, knot magic
- **Season** - Winter
- **Celtic name** - Tuath
- **Hour of the day** - Midnight
- **Alchemical symbol** - upside-down triangle while having a line in the middle
- **Symbols** - Caves, fields, gems, rocks, mountains
- **Symbolic creatures** - Stag, bull, sphinx
- **Plants** - Thrift plant, red poppy, grains, ivy

Air

Air strongly connects to the mind, intelligence, and mental process. This element is creative and works in such a way that it can lead to the manifestation of your magical intentions. You can also see it as having a strong connection with wisdom, higher consciousness, purification, and divination.

It also symbolizes inspiration, communication, clarity, freedom, ideas, dreams and wishes, and the capacity to know and understand, among many others. Some rituals related to air require you to toss a few objects in the wind, play a wind instrument or flute, hang certain objects in high places or trees, and burn aromatherapy and incense.

- **Direction** – East
- **Color** – Blue
- **Qualities** – light and active, hot and moist
- **Metal** – Mercury, aluminum, tin
- **Zodiac signs** – Libra, Gemini, Aquarius
- **Types of magic** – Finding a lost or stolen object, divination, visualization, magic of four winds
- **Season** – Spring
- **Celtic name** – Airt
- **Hour of the day** – Dawn
- **Alchemical symbol** – right side up triangle while having a line in the middle
- **Symbols** – Wind, sky, incense, clouds
- **Symbolic creatures** – Hawk, eagle, butterfly
- **Plants** – Mistletoe, aspen tree

Fire

The fire element is also important in the world of magic as it is a symbol of change, inspiration, energy, life force, passion, sexuality, love, faith, trust, leadership, spirit, innocence, elusiveness, and will. It symbolizes self-healing, renewal, personal and physical vulnerability, protection, and relationship with yourself and others.

The fire element also has a link to passion and change. It is spiritual and physical, as it is linked to both divinity and sexuality. You can also expect fire magic to quickly fill and manifest with primal energy.

- **Direction** – South
- **Color** – Red
- **Qualities** – light and active, hot and dry
- **Metal** – Gold, brass, steel, iron
- **Zodiac signs** – Aries, Sagittarius, Leo
- **Types of magic** – Healing, tantra, candle magic

- **Season** – Summer
- **Celtic name** – Deas
- **Hour of the day** – Noon
- **Alchemical symbol** – right side up triangle
- **Symbols** – Fire, volcanoes, stars, sun, hearth fire, candle flame
- **Symbolic creatures** – fire-breathing dragons, lions, horses
- **Plants** – Red poppies, onions, garlic, nettle

Water

The water element represents feelings, absorption, purification, intuition, unconscious/subconscious mind, courage, emotions, wisdom, self-healing, psychic ability, reflection, vision quests, and eternal movement. It also encompasses every emotional aspect of femininity and love.

The water element strongly relates to your intuition, emotions, and subconscious mind. Since it is a primal component of life, the womb symbolizes this element and makes it relevant to fertility. As for the rituals you can do with the aid of the water element, some examples are ritual bathing, tossing some objects into water, sprinkling, washing, diluting, and brewing.

- **Direction** – West
- **Color** – Green
- **Qualities** – Heavy and passive, cold and moist
- **Metal** – Silver, copper
- **Zodiac signs** – Scorpio, Cancer, Pisces
- **Types of magic** – Mirror magic, healing, purification, fertility, dream magic, divination
- **Season** – Fall
- **Celtic name** – Iar
- **Hour of the day** – Twilight
- **Alchemical symbol** – Upside down triangle
- **Symbols** – Bodies of water, rain, waterfalls, fog, waves
- **Symbolic creatures** – All water creatures, snakes, scorpions, dragons or serpents, dolphin

- **Plants** - All water plants, lotus, fern, moss

Spirit

Lastly, there is what we call the spirit element. It is almost identical to the fire element. Note that there are times when spiritual entities, like nature spirits, ancestors, and Gods, become recognized as spiritual elements in ritual. It also represents most things considered spiritual, including goddesses, omnipresence, immanence, transcendence, and the center of the universe.

- **Direction** - Center
- **Color** - White, purple, black, rainbow
- **Qualities** - Being spaceless, timelessness
- **Metal** - Meteorite
- **Season** - Cycle itself
- **Time** - Beyond time, solar and lunar cycles
- **Symbols** - Spiral, the cosmos
- **Symbolic creatures** - Sphinx, owl

The Moon Phases and Their Importance

Aside from the mentioned elemental correspondences, you should know that moon phases and sun energy will play a crucial role in spellcrafting and making magic. All witches and witchcraft practitioners fully know how powerful moon phases are. They have used these moon phases ever since to give them courage, guidance, success, and luck in crafting and casting spells.

They also use the power of the moon phases to heighten the power of their spellwork. The fact that the moon is a heavenly body, which is the closest to the sky, also means that it can greatly influence your life and the results of your spellwork. If you want to practice witchcraft, you can use the moon phases when timing your magic. Doing so can increase the power of your spells.

Here are the primary moon phases to guide you in timing your magic. Each of these moon phases has its own special energies and power.

New Moon (Phase 1)

Considered the first phase, the new moon serves as a representation of a fresh start. The moon in the first phase is hardly visible as the sky may look black. There are instances when magic is quite literal, so while the moon is in the phase wherein it is not visible, it is the perfect time to perform shadow work. You can also use this phase to recognize your dark sides or hide or shadow yourself.

For example, you are aware that you are somewhat manipulative. Still, whenever someone calls you out about it, you feel the need to defend yourself or deny the presence of such a trait. In this case, you can use the new moon to explore your shadow side (for example. your manipulative side) and look for ways you can positively work with it.

It is the perfect time to look for healthy ways to use such skills, like building a much better career without the risk of hurting others. You may also want to use your manipulative side to read others to convince your partner of the importance of communicating together instead of being the only one in control.

The fact that the new moon represents new beginnings also means that it is the perfect moment to set your intentions and goals for the next cycle. This first phase should encourage beginnings, like falling in love. To set yourself off to a new beginning, you need to release yourself from the past.

Let go of everything that happened in the past, especially negative ones. The new moon will always have your back anytime you wish to clear the path of your love life and remove all the bad energies in it. This is a good thing in your attempt to find your ideal mate.

- **Rising and setting time** - Dawn and sunset
- **Time** - From the first time the new moon appears and three and a half days after
- **Pagan Holiday** - Winter solstice
- **Purpose** - Beginnings
- **Offering** - Milk and honey
- **Theme** - Abundance
- **Magic** - Divination, health, deconstructive magic and curses, business, love, self-improvement, beauty

Waxing Moon (Phase 2)

In this phase, expect the moon to become luminous literally. It will look like a fascinating orb appearing in the sky. The waxing moon phase serves as the time for you to prioritize the specific areas of your life that you have longed to focus on, like personal aspects, including empathy, self-discovery, and love. Reflect on the things that make you completely happy.

Focus on crafting spells for your personal betterment and improving your sense of happiness and fulfillment. Also, note that during this phase, the waxing moon tends to grow and become even brighter. It, therefore, creates a perfect phase for you to perform sympathetic magic surrounding growth.

The energy the waxing moon provides can also support you when it comes to attracting, drawing, constructing, and manifesting things to yourself. That said, you can use these energies in crafting spells for improvement, like in areas of spiritual growth, career, finance, love, job opportunities, creativity, and positivity.

- **Rising and setting time** – Mid-morning and sunset
- **Time** – Three and a half to seven days after the new moon came out
- **Pagan Holiday** – Imbolc
- **Purpose** – Movement of things
- **Offering** – Candles
- **Theme** – Manifestation
- **Magic** – Animal magic, attraction spells, friendships, inner beauty, protection, success, luck, wealth, healing, psychic work, change, emotions

Full Moon (Phase 3)

Many consider this third phase, the full moon, as the strongest out of all the moon phases. In astrology, the full moon comes out when the moon and the sun are on opposing sides. During this phase, expect a lot of emotions to run high, making everything all the more intense.

The good news is that you can take advantage of this intensity by making it a part of your spells while knowing that there is a bright ball of power that continues to shine upon you and help you. Some practitioners even make it a point to charge their crystals during this phase. They just put their crystals in a spot that gets them exposed to the light shone by the full moon.

You can also create full-moon water. All you have to do is put a glass of water in a place where the full moon's light shines on it. Make it a point to put the glass or goblet containing the water above your letter of intention.

Leave the water there so the full moon can charge it. You may then use the full moon water as part of your spells and rituals.

Also, note that the intensity of the full moon may cause you to feel extremely heavy in case there are certain emotional issues that you are currently avoiding or processing. That said, honor what your body is telling you during this time. If you feel it is asking for more rest and sleep, give it that.

- **Rising and setting time** – Sunset and dawn
- **Time** – Fourteen to seventeen days and a half after the new moon appeared
- **Pagan Holiday** – Summer solstice
- **Purpose** – Project completion
- **Offering** – Flowers
- **Theme** – Power
- **Magic** – Health, beauty, divination, healing, fitness, psychic work, romance, banishing, love, dreams, change, protection, motivation, family, money, psychic work, clarity

Waning Moon (Phase 4)

The waning moon refers to the period when the moon becomes darker again. It moves from the full moon and then back to the new moon. In this fourth phase, you can perform banishing work. For instance, you could cut cords with a lover in the past. Note, though, that banishing a specific person completely from your life is not the only thing you can do under this phase.

You can also perform other powerful banishing spells, like those that eliminate your toxic or bad feelings for someone. You can also work on banishing your self-doubts and insecurities when the waning moon phase comes. It is an incredible moment to empower yourself instead of changing another's will.

You can use it to eliminate anything that you consider negative, toxic, or bad for you, including unfair treatment in the workplace or your imposter syndrome. Get rid of unwanted negativities, particularly those that tend to keep you from enjoying and living your life to the fullest.

Reflect on things that block you from reaching your goals. Pay attention to energy and roadblocks so you can release yourself from anything hindering you from attaining your desired goals.

- **Rising and setting time** – Mid-evening and Mid-morning
- **Time** – Three and a half to seven days after the full moon appeared
- **Pagan Holiday** – Lammas
- **Purpose** – Initial destruction
- **Offering** – Rice or grain
- **Theme** – Reassessment
- **Magic** – Addictions, emotions, banishing, cleansing, divorce, protection, undoing curses and bindings

Dark Moon (Phase 5)

Lastly, there is the dark moon, a particularly powerful moon phase that occurs before the next lunar cycle. All spells during this special moon phase have to be well-thought-out. This phase is a time to work on something bigger than you – one that is beyond what is personal. It should let you deal with bigger situations and concerns involving more than one person, like in the case of divorce, death, or addiction.

For instance, if you have bad habits, like smoking, that you want to get rid of, then the dark moon phase is the best time for you to do it. You can create a spell designed to strengthen your willpower so you will succeed in quitting your unwanted habits.

It is also in the dark moon wherein you can reflect deeply on your passion and anger while asking for strength and compassion. You can perform dark moon spells in 10 and ½ to 14 days after the full moon's arrival.

Some witches avoid casting spells during the dark moon. However, others consider it as the best time for workings. In terms of magic, the dark moon is designed for divination. Aside from banishing unhelpful and unwanted habits, you can also banish spells during this phase to eliminate energies and relationships.

A lot of witches also take advantage of the dark moon phase to do spells linked to completely removing something from their life. Some also use it to cleanse so they will come fully prepared for the new moon.

The Sun Energy and Its Importance in Spellcrafting

In a lot of Pagan traditions at present, you will likely notice them putting more emphasis on the power, energies, and magic of the moon. It is not the only heavenly body you can take advantage of regarding spellcrafting and witchcraft.

While sometimes ignored and taken for granted, the sun is extremely important in spells, especially if you consider it a source of magic, myth, and legend for several decades.

Similar to the moon, the sun also has its own cycles. Basically, there are two cycles for the sun, namely, the day and the year. Also called the wheel of the year, the yearly cycle works by increasing the sun's power until Litha (when it reaches its peak power). After that, the sun's power leaks off as the wheel approaches the spectrum of darkness.

Some find the daily sun cycle more convenient. In this cycle, you will notice the sun's power increasing until noontime when it reaches the peak point in the sky. Upon falling towards the horizon, expect the power of the sun to wane. As for the sunset, many consider it a liminal time. It signifies that the sunset is visible in between two worlds.

Summer Sun Energies

When the summer months come, the sun's energy will become most efficient for specific classifications and categories of working. It is like when the waxing moon comes with different intentions from those of the waning moon. Sure, you can do all sorts of magic any time you wish, but remember that your spellwork will be more efficient when you perfect your timing.

Generally, the summer creates sure and strong energy; logically, it follows that performing magic about health, healing, and beauty will be more effective during this time. It also assists greatly in spells promoting love and other relationships.

If you wish to restart a project, you can use the summer sun as your ultimate energy source. One important fact to remember is that the summer sun energies tend to change as time passes. With that, expect them to be divided based on sun signs, namely Leo, Virgo, and Cancer.

Cancer

Starting from the 22nd of June to the 23rd of July, there's a chance for Cancer energies to be at their strongest or peak. "Home and Hearth" are the themes for this time of year. In other words, your family, your closest relationships, and your abode. This is the optimum time for spellwork regarding your emotions.

Leo

The Lion (July to August 22) encompasses strength and courage, creativity and showmanship, willpower, and fertility. Use his energies wisely and copiously for success.

Strongly linked to physical appearances, Leo is particularly helpful when trying for a healthy and beautiful glow - and for weight loss. Last - but not least - use Leo's energies to work on pride (the good kind), generosity of heart, and ambitiousness (again, the good kind!)

Virgo

Virgo is the last component of summer, from around the 23rd of August to the 22nd of September. The energy and vibe of this sign demonstrate self-improvement, organization, and service. You can also make Virgo energies work for you if there is a certain problem you have to analyze.

For instance, if your goal is to contribute to solving global issues, such as poverty or hunger, then you should consider doing it during this specific period. Virgo also contributes to dealing with certain issues that revolve around your health, mental energies, ability to pay attention to detail, responsibilities, and employment.

Daily Sun Cycle

If you want to take advantage of the sun's daily cycle, learning about the following phases composing the cycle can help.

Sunrise

Most feel at their freshest and highest level of energy upon waking up in the morning. With that, it is the best time to do magical work. Note that the morning sun will always serve as an incredible source of energy. You may want to begin your day with a ritual, which contributes to making you feel at your best even more.

Cast your charms in the morning's sun to rid yourself of the negative energies floating around you. This is also the time best time to fight addictions.

With its ability to start your day, the morning sun works best for any form of magic concerning those you can begin in the morning, such as school or business.

Midday

The midday involves the sun energies after lunchtime. It is considered the highest point or peak in the sky, considering that the sun's energy level is at its highest at this time of the day. With the great strength of the sun during midday, you can use it to overcome all weaknesses you intend to get rid of. You can cast your spell at lunchtime under the bright and high sun in case you want to be inspired or guided.

Sunset

As for the sunset, it is certainly a special time of the day. It is when the colors you can see above the sky promote the cooling of the ground. The ground also tends to cool down as the sunset comes with darkness and a soft breeze. The dusk will always be the perfect moment for relaxation. It will boost your willpower, serenity, and calmness.

Also considered "a liminal time," sunset is a time between worlds, allowing for unbelievable magic to take place! Between day and night, this liminal time is perfect for adjusting to changes.

Chapter 3 – The Spellcrafter's Toolkit

As a beginner in crafting and casting spells - and the world of magic and witchcraft in general - among the first few things that you may be wondering about is the specific tools you need to create your own spells and cast them. There are several tools that a spellcrafter can use. Note, though, that all the recommended special tools are not one hundred percent necessary.

The reason is that, in reality, it would be unnecessary to use any special tools since the magic relies on the actual practitioner. Also, witchcraft and spellcrafting revolve around meanings. This means that the tools you should use have a specific meaning and identity that you can uniquely link to. The connection is what will provide you with the power you need for the practice.

You have to know the importance of every ingredient and tool used in crafting and casting spells. By doing that, you can successfully form magic rituals and spells that you can use in building a path designed to make your life more meaningful and spiritual.

Over time, the tools you decide to use for all your spells will be a major part of you. They will help define your identity as a spellcrafter and witchcraft practitioner. You can also use such tools in your journey toward becoming a real maker of spells.

Essential Tools for Spellcrafting

To give you an idea, here are some useful tools for spellcrafting and spellcasting.

Athame

Athame refers to a dagger or knife that you can use for ritual purposes. It is conventionally a double-bladed knife that features a black handle. You should never use it for cutting anything, though. It should be exclusive for directing your desired energy during your ritual. One example is when commanding and summoning spirits and elementals.

The athame is also classified as a projective tool symbolizing the air when you think about it based on the classical elements' system. You must put it on your altar, specifically on the East side.

Upon deciding on your athame, you can start customizing it using a meaningful symbol. Make sure to choose a symbol that represents you or has a meaning for you. For example, you can draw a pentagram in it or inscribe your name. You can put any symbol you want on the athame, provided it truly has a special meaning for you.

Bell

Another useful tool and instrument that you can use for spellcrafting is the bell. It is a spiritual musical instrument you can play when evoking positive energies, indicating the start or end of various parts of your rituals, or summoning deities or spirits. The sound produced by the bell is sacred, so it will only be useful every time you get into the ritual mental state.

You can also find those who use Tibetan drums or bowls in place of the bell. One reason behind using such instruments is that it helps create an action in the world that is different from your daily actions.

Broom

While there are legends about flying witches riding on their brooms, the one you can use in crafting spells and your rituals is a misunderstood magical instrument. Contrary to what others believe (that it is a bad instrument used by witches), the main purpose of the broom that we are talking about here is to clean only.

Note, though, that you can't use it for cleaning materially or physically. What it is going to clean is the energy. It works in purifying your sacred environment before the actual opening of the circle.

Due to its purifying and cleaning purposes, many associate it with the water element. You can also use it in love spells as well as spells designed to improve your psychic powers. Many practitioners also believe that hanging a broom behind a door can help protect a house from negativity and evil spells.

Traditionally, you need to use the actual broom but note that you can also make your own. Use ash to create the stick, then tie broom or birch branches together with the help of a willow.

Wand

When directing energies, you can also use the wand – which is an invocation instrument. It symbolizes the air element and must be around 15 to 20 inches long. The wand can also be made using any type of wood, including willow, oak, peach, and cherry.

Certain versions of wands are also constructed from crystal, metal, or stone. The material used in creating the wand will depend on the specific purpose for which you intend to use it. It would be best to use the wand for your spells and rituals during the spring, specifically at sunset or dawn or at midnight or noon every Wednesday.

Cauldron

The cauldron is a symbol of water and the Goddess. Traditionally, it should use iron material for its construction and should be around three feet on its base. The cauldron should also have a narrower opening compared to the rest of its body.

If your cauldron is small enough, it would be a great instrument for ritual cooking and for cooking herbal teas. The cauldron also seems to serve another role or purpose when placed on your altar. When performing spring rituals, for instance, you can fill it up with flowers and water.

It is, therefore, safe to assume that the cauldron serves as a valuable container for every consecrated object. You can also use it as a container for your burnt offerings to the gods.

You need to light up a small fire inside the cauldron during winter rituals. Just be cautious whenever you decide to burn or light up something in the cauldron to guarantee your safety.

Chalice

The chalice refers to a cup that features a long stem. You can fill up the chalice with a wide range of liquids every time you perform rituals or cast spells. In most cases, the chalice is meant to hold water, the element represented by the tool, which has to be on the altar all the time.

Aside from that, the chalice is also a tool you can use to pour wine during ritual toasts and Sabbat offerings, as well as blood and other liquid forms based on what exact spell you intend to make or cast. It is also possible to use a chalice to mix salt and water, so you can trace not only the protective circle but also purifications and blessings.

The chalice useful in spellcrafting and casting is constructed from different materials – among which are brass, silver, ceramic, stone, and glass. You can pick any of the materials you want your chalice to be based on.

Several groups in Wiccan tradition also hold two chalices – one used for cleaning water while the other for the wine and any other form of liquid. When in a coven, you need a main chalice that you can carry into the altar to allow consecrations. You must also share this cup with every member during the ceremony.

Some Wiccans also make it a point to garnish the chalices they are using with symbols or runes for decorating purposes. Others also paint the chalice or attach a semi-precious stone. That way, it will begin containing and providing energy to any liquid that's within the chalice.

Candles

You also need candles; many practitioners consider these as having an extremely vital role in rituals. One reason is that these candles can help create the best state of mind. The color, presence, and aroma of candles work to put you in a good mood.

What's great about choosing the perfect candles for your spells is that they can encourage feelings of love, prosperity, and health. Make it a point to store several candles of any color at home. That way, you no longer have to spend much time looking for a candle before casting your spells.

Altar

The look of the altar does not matter that much in most cases. The most important thing here is the base material, which has to be based on metal or wood. It is also important to set it up so that it contains everything you need for the spell or ritual.

Once you have an altar, prepare a cloth that comes in a color that perfectly suits the ritual or spell you intend to perform. You can then use it as a covering for your altar. Moreover, you should put the Gods' symbols on your altar.

For instance, you can put on a white and black candle to symbolize the mother and father, respectively. Other items you can put on the altar are the wand, bell, cauldron, athame, censer, and any other material or offering for the rite.

Libation Bowl

The libation bowl refers to a dedicated container that you can use to hold a libation, a drink or beverage you can pour out as an offering to the spirit, beloved dead, and deity in a ritual context. One thing to note about libations is that they differ based on traditions.

You can even classify alcoholic beverages, oil, water, honey, and milk as libations. Once inside the libation bowl, it is safe to use it for pouring the drink so you can start offering it to the appropriate spirits and deities.

Scrying Bowl

Scrying is the primary divination strategy that a lot of people are already aware of. It is an ancient divination art with the primary goal of gaining information. You can also often achieve the best results from scrying just by gazing upon or into a reflective surface or a crystal. Let your eyes relax as you gaze into the objects.

Let your inner psychic open so it can receive the information and visions you desire. With the help of scrying tools, like the scrying bowl, you have a higher chance of attaining the mental state needed to enter a trance, serving as the focal point of visualization. You can also use other tools you can see here, like mirrors, polished precious stones, water, and crystal balls.

Cord/Thread

You may also want to use a cord or thread when planning to work with knot magic. Along with the cord and thread, ribbons and strings are primary ingredients in creating and casting knot magic, a process that requires you to tie or bind together.

You may also use black thread in making dolls in other traditions. Moreover, thread is a big help in sewing mojo bags by hand. This will let you create mojo bags that you can also transform into an amulet.

Incense Charcoal

Charcoal refers to the safest and easiest way of burning incense. Use it in cleansing your home. It is ideal for use along with frankincense, palo santo, loose white sage, and copal. After each use, be prepared to handle a lot of ash, but you can rest assured that you can easily dispose of them.

Pentacle

The pentacle is characterized by a 5-pointed star within a circle representing the Earth. It is a protective and evocative tool for spellcrafting and witchcraft, designed to keep your place protected from any form of harm while removing negativity. You can hang this pentacle on your window or doors to protect yourself from any negative energy when performing a ritual. It is also helpful in evoking positive energies. To make the most out of the pentacle, it would be best to bless and consecrate it before each use.

How to Cleanse and Consecrate Magical Tools?

Before using your ritual tools for your spells and rituals, it would be best to customize, cleanse and consecrate them. The process of personalizing, cleansing, and consecrating your tools is even more significant if your ritual tools are purchased instead of being created by you.

The consecration and cleansing process is necessary because it purifies your magical tools before you use them for interacting with the divine. Aside from that, it helps in getting rid of all negative energies that are in the tool. It comes in handy if you are unsure of the past history of the tool or the previous owner before you get a hold of it.

Cleansing

Cleansing your magical tools, as its name suggests, is all about cleaning and purifying them. However, it is also different in the sense that you will not be cleaning the item physically. What you will be doing here is to clean it spiritually, meaning based on its current energy level.

With the help of cleansing, you can disassociate the tools or items used for your magic and spells from their previous vibrations. Note that all the activities that the items went through cause them to collect bits of energy. It could be from when it was still sitting in a store or factory, in transport, sitting on a shelf, or being handled by people.

When the tool reaches you, you may want to focus on wiping its vibrational slate clean. This is so you can keep it attuned to the specific energies you are emitting or the ones that align with your goal.

To cleanse the magical tool/object, follow these simple steps.

- Prepare a cleansing incense – One example is sage. Once you have this incense around, you should burn it, then run the tool

through the smoke emitted by the incense.
- After that, bury the tool for a while - Burying the tool in the earth or a bowl containing cornmeal, salt, or dirt will work for that purpose.
- Prepare saltwater - Soak the tool in it. You may also spray or sprinkle your magical tool with salt water.
- Hold the tool for a short period beneath running water - Wave the tool over the flame emitted by a candle, then put it into the fire.
- Use a blessed broom (besom) to sweep away all negative energies.

When doing the steps, you have to be cautious and practical. Be extra careful when following the steps and ensure that what you are doing perfectly fits the material you are cleansing and handling. For instance, if your magical tool is made of metal, you should avoid soaking it in saltwater overnight; otherwise, it will risk developing rust. Also, avoid putting a fabric pouch containing several herbs close to a fire.

Use your sense of judgment whenever you are cleansing to guarantee your safety. Aim to do the process of cleansing new magical tools before using them for rituals and other spiritual purposes or cleansing already existing tools, like crystals, altar tools, and jewelry, especially if you are using them a lot, while prioritizing your safety. Cleansing is also necessary for magical and spellcrafters tools that sit unused for a long time.

Consecrating

After cleansing, you should consecrate your magical tools. The consecration process is all about making your magical tools sacred using minor acts of blessing or rites. It requires you to elevate the purpose of your magical tools into a spiritual one by performing the art of blessing. Any tool you intend to use is suitable for consecration, including jewelry items and other tools. You can even consecrate the ground beneath your house.

Note, though, that once you consecrate the tool, you should start treating it accordingly, as it is already sacred. Some steps you should take when consecrating an item are indicated next.

- Say a prayer over the magical tool. Dedicate your use of it to the Gods and its intended purpose.

- Use cleansed, consecrated, and charged oils to anoint your magical tool/s.
- Consecrate the tool using the elements of earth, water, fire, and air when performing a blessing ritual – What you should do is run the tool through the smoke of incense. Have some salt sprinkled on it, then let the tool pass through the flame. After that, sprinkle some water on it.
- Increase the tool's intent to perform the good work executed by the abundant universe.

Charging

Apart from cleansing and consecrating, you may also want to add the crucial process of charging your magical tools. When you charge your tools, you mainly empower them with appropriate energy. You may want to imbue the tools with positivity or have them charged in such a way that their vibrations start to become aligned with a certain intention.

Charging requires you to raise your own level of energy to direct it to your magical tools. You can choose a charging method based on what you prefer and the specific tool/s you are charging.

Here are some effective methods of charging your spellcrafter and magical tools.

- Dancing, chanting, or meditating – This should help raise the tool's power and then pour such energy imaginatively into it using a song, targeted or focused intent, or movement.
- Doing a small ritual should aim to increase energy and intent while keeping you invested in your item.
- Performing visualization – This helps transmit intent and energy to your tools, after which you can release them so that the tool can perform its intended function.

Note that you can also develop something that is only yours. You can create it in such a way that you can accomplish your goal based on your belief system.

Basic Layout for your Altar

The altar is the focal point of all your spellwork and rituals. This means that it is unique since it is going to be you who will design and customize it based on your personality and the spells you intend to make and cast.

Also, note that from one witch, ritual, and even spell to another, it is highly likely for the altar to be dynamic. It changes all the time. This is what makes the altar remain alive and keeps the energy flowing.

Therefore, the altar's layout - while having basic components - is going to be up to the witchcraft practitioner. Also, note that your main purpose for practicing can greatly affect the entire layout, shape, and size.

It is easy and simple to set up a basic altar. It often just requires any table where you can put the tools you intend to use and the symbols that depict your beliefs. An important rule is to feel free to explore, decorate, redecorate/rearrange the components of your altar. Do not forget to have fun while creating or setting up your altar.

Before putting an item on the altar, make sure that you study its meaning first. Also, reflect on the specific reasons why you like to use the item or tool and how to use it effectively. Avoid cluttering your altar, too. Remember that your altar also serves as your workspace, so there should be enough room and space for all your tools and ingredients.

Make it a point to empty it when unused. Do not clutter it by setting an actual place for you to put and organize your tools. It could be on a shelf, box, or drawer - anywhere you can safely put them away.

Decorating Your Altar

To give you an idea of how you can lay out and decorate your altar, we are going to talk about its most common components.

Altar Cloth

Regardless of the altar you intend to create, you should cover the surface with a cloth. This should serve as an ornamental piece that protects the table from scratches, wax drippings, and liquids. Shop for a cloth that you can use for your altar. If there is one that catches your interest that also has a symbol in it, inquire about the actual meaning.

Find out if it is truly meaningful for you before buying it and using it on your altar. If you are up to it, you can also make your cloth. You can change the cloth based on the kind of ritual you intend to do. The changes may depend on the season and the Pagan holiday you are celebrating.

Religious Symbols

You may want to put some religious symbols on your altar if you are a practitioner who strongly connects to Hinduism, Buddhism, Christianity, or any other spiritual tradition. In this case, you may put some figures and images symbolizing your beliefs that also remind you of who you really are.

Are you devoted to a certain deity? Then you may also put a drawing or statue symbolizing that deity on your altar. If you consider yourself a Wiccan, you can put a pentagram in the middle of the altar.

Candle Holder

You need the candle holder as part of your altar decoration if you have plans to work with candle magic. Ensure that you have at least one of these holders. Your choice of a candle holder also needs to be strong and sturdy enough to withstand the candle's heat without easily falling over in case you accidentally bump into the altar. Choose eco-friendly and biodegradable tools, too. Among the best materials for the candle holder are glass, metal, and ceramics.

Incense Burner

The incense burner is also important for your altar if you intend to cast a spell. This burner is available in several styles and shapes. You may also put a cauldron on the altar to let you burn some herbs for your spells and rituals.

Creating the Altar

Based on the mentioned components, note that the altar has building blocks in the form of its four traditional elements – all of which you can align with the help of four cardinal points. As an example, here is a layout of a basic altar that spellcrafters use.

- A bowl containing sand, plant, or dirt is positioned on the altar's North end– This should represent the earth element.
- Stick of incense – Put it in the East to symbolize the air element.
- Charcoal or candle – Position it in the South to represent the fire element.
- Bowl or glass with water – Make sure it faces the east to represent the water element.

Light the candle and incense every time you need to craft or cast spells or during rituals. Be extra careful, though. Never leave burning candles behind without you around. In case you need to go somewhere, blow it out.

Chapter 4 – Getting Started with Ritual

Now, it is time for you to start your spells and rituals. Before starting, you should remember how serious each spell or ritual is. You need to be prepared for it physically and mentally, so if you are still underaged or someone who is still battling with a mental health issue, you have to avoid it.

If you are fully certain you can handle the spellwork and ritual, you should start preparing for it. Remember that unless you prepare for it properly and appropriately, it will be impossible for you to make it produce the result you want. You must do meticulous preparation while adhering to instructions to ensure that your rituals and spells will work based on how you intend them to.

Selecting the Perfect Ritual Location

One of the first things you should do when preparing for the spellcrafting ritual is the location. It serves as your magic space where you can hold your ritual, so select this space carefully. You need the right location for your ritual as it contributes greatly to attaining your intended result.

Pick a space that has a certain calm. It should be a place that will not disturb you in any way, especially when you are either crafting or casting your spells. Note, though, that you still have to plan for any unexpected interruptions in advance, so you will know what to do in case those come, no matter how careful you are.

The ideal ritual location is outdoors. It should be in a quiet and natural environment that is close to the earth. It could be in a meadow, field, forest, or any location that is close to the water or trees.

However, keep in mind that you will be unable to hold the ritual outdoors all the time. The most convenient place would still be in your home. In that case, look for a spot in your home with sufficient calmness and quietness. It should let you hold your rituals without any disturbance. Moreover, it needs to have sufficient space so you can cast the circle needed for all forms of ritual.

Cleansing your Magical or Sacred Space

Once you have chosen your ritual space, it is time to cleanse it. Cleansing is necessary before crafting and casting any spell, as it will help rid your space of negative vibrations and energies. The good news is that there are many ways for you to do the cleansing – some of which will be discussed briefly next.

Ritual

This cleansing method requires using rock salt, four white fabric bags, and sea salt. Mix the salts, then put the mixture inside the bags. Put each bag in every corner of your sacred space so you can completely cleanse it. While putting the bag, say this spell.

I am cleansing this sacred space

I am commanding every negative force and vibration

To get out of this place

So mote it be

Visualize the negative energies and vibrations leaving your sacred or magical space while you say the statement. You may also smudge this space using sage.

Smudging

For this specific cleansing method, you will need a smudge stick. In this case, the most suitable for use are sweetgrass, sage, frankincense, and cedar. Here are the steps for using the smudge stick.

- Light the smudge stick – Continue lighting it until it burns – after which you should blow it out. Expect the stick to continue producing smoke, which is what you should aim for.

- Walk starting in the east – This means walking the whole space following a clockwise motion starting from the east. Your goal here is to smudge the entire space.
- Visualize all the negative vibrations and energies leaving your sacred space as you do the smudging.

Sweeping

The simple act of sweeping your entire space is also an effective way to cleanse your sacred space. This requires the use of the besom or broom, which is specifically designed for magical uses.

- Sweep your entire sacred space – Begin in the east and do it clockwise.
- Clean the air symbolically – To do that, just lift the besom as high as possible.
- As you sweep, visualize the negative vibrations and energies finally saying goodbye from your space.

Cleansing Yourself

Apart from your sacred space, you must also cleanse yourself in preparation for the ritual. Spend time before the ritual to choose a special bath salt, herbal bath, or soap for the pre-ritual cleansing. It is unnecessary to take the cleansing bath before the actual ritual if you do not prefer to do so. Doing it one night before is okay if you think it fits better with your lifestyle and schedule.

When preparing for the cleansing bath, note that you are also allowed to select the ornaments. You can add candles to the area. You may also pour a few drops of your chosen essential oils into the water you will use.

If you have crystals, you can also put them around your bathtub. Be extra cautious when using crystals around water, though. The reason is that some of them, such as lapis lazuli, kyanite, malachite, and selenite, should never be directly exposed to salt water or pure water. If you wish to use the crystals for your cleansing bath, study them first to guarantee your safety.

In addition to the spiritual cleansing ritual bath that you can do by taking a bath in water that you infuse with flowers, salts, teas, crystal vibrations, herbs, and crystals, among many others, you may also choose to do self-cleansing rituals using other means.

- Smudging Ritual - This requires you to use the smoke that comes out of certain herbs so you can cleanse your aura. Among the herbs you can use for this self-cleansing smudging ritual are sweetgrass, cedar, sage, palo santo, and rosemary.
- Crystal Ritual - Here, you will need to use a wand with a high-vibrational crystal, like selenite. You should let the wand pass over your body to remove all negative vibrations and energies.
- Asperging (blessing) using blessed or holy water - This method requires you to spray or spritz the blessed or holy water over your body. Make sure that you cover each part of yourself, from your head down to your feet. Aside from the actual holy water, you may also use rose water and moon water, among others.
- Energetic cleansing - This requires the use of divine healing energies, like Reiki, to cleanse yourself.

Another method, though not highly recommended as it involves the use of fire that may lead to accidents if you are not careful, is bonfire cleansing. It is a ritual that requires you to pass through a couple of bonfires or leap over one to have yourself cleansed.

Wearing Appropriate Colors

Preparing for the ritual also involves wearing the appropriate colors for it. Note that color energy will always be a vital aspect of every ritual work, so you should make it a part of your preparation. Pick clothing or any other adornment depending on the kind of energy you intend to create in your sacred space. Take a look at these colors to guide you.

- Black - designed for transformation and the releasing and banishing of negative energies
- White - understanding, cleansing, finding clarity, building order, spiritual growth
- Orange - power and encouragement
- Red - health rituals and love spells
- Blue - intensifying psychic abilities and healing rituals
- Green - good luck, prosperity, money spells, employment spells, and fertility rituals
- Yellow - divination and communication spells

- Brown – home rituals, grounding and balance
- Violet – balance and divination
- Gray – complex decision-making and binding any negative influence
- Silver – meditation, the release of negativity, psychic development
- Pink – romance and love spells, kid's magic, and spiritual awakening
- Gold – divination, spells for good fortune, success, and health
- Indigo – meditation and spiritual healing

In addition to the color of your clothing, it is also advisable to use freshly washed and clean ones. Remember that you may be staying in an awkward or unusual pose when performing the ritual for a prolonged period, so choose comfortable clothing that blends well with the present weather.

Gathering the Right Materials

Another important thing to do is to use the best materials that are the most appropriate for the spell you intend to make. Note that various oils, herbs, and candles may be necessary to effectively execute the ritual or spell. The spell's progress may get damaged if you use inappropriate and incorrect materials.

Every ingredient also possesses certain power and energy that works specifically for your goal. Yes, indeed, advanced practitioners are already skilled enough that they can substitute certain materials and ingredients. However, since you are still a beginner, it is not advisable to do so. Make it a point to get the right materials, prepare them for the ritual, and spell appropriately.

Once you have gathered the materials needed for your spell, start setting them out depending on the specific manner through which they are guaranteed to work. For instance, if you use certain candles, you may have to use a special oil first to anoint them. It may also be necessary to put the candles in a specific formation to radiate the correct energy.

If you are using herbs, you may have to burn or consume them in a specific way that helps harness their full potency. For tools and crystals, cleansing and charging them may be necessary. You can do all the steps necessary to prepare your materials during the planning stage. By doing that, you are assured that every material and tool you need is ready for what's ahead once it is time to perform the actual ritual or spell.

Preparing your Mental State

Another important aspect of ritual preparation is your mental state. You have to keep yourself attuned to the ritual since it will be you who has the primary role in the process. This is where you should remind yourself that you should avoid holding rituals, crafting spells, casting spells, or performing any other magical work in case you are experiencing some issues affecting your mental state.

It could be that you feel unwell or sick, or you are mentally unstable or emotionally agitated, probably because of anger and grief. It could also be that your intuition is telling you that you should not do the ritual or magical work at that particular time. In that particular case, you have to listen to what your intuition is telling you.

You may also want to follow the technique of other spellcasters and witches who tend to fast before performing the ritual. They do so as they feel like it will be a big help in internally cleansing themselves, thereby keeping them free as much as possible.

You should also avoid drinking alcohol or using any drug or unwanted substances 12 hours or so before the scheduled ritual. The goal here is to keep your mind as clear as possible so you can bring it to its absolute peak as far as its strength is concerned.

It is also advisable to spend at least half an hour preparing yourself mentally before the actual ritual. Look at yourself internally. Focus on yourself and the ritual or magical work you are about to execute. Ensure that you are clear regarding what you want from the ritual and how you intend it to work.

Aside from that, set yourself free from all the things that bother and hinder you. Give yourself the kind of internal purification that you need. Imagine the dissipation of all your negative energies and influences, including your anger and stress.

You should then make room for the coming of the white flame that tends to burn brightly inside you. Once you feel like you are already calm, relaxed, and strong, then you are truly prepared to begin and do your ritual.

How to Cast the Circle

The circle we are talking about here frequently refers to a barrier that houses your rituals and spells. You need to cast this circle before your rituals and spells to ensure that you have allocated more than enough energy to protect yourself from negative and unwanted outside influences. The good thing about casting a circle is that you can do it in many ways - some are formal, while others are informal.

Traditionally, casting a circle may involve calling upon a goddess or a god. However, suppose you consider yourself a secular witch. What you will most likely be calling upon would be the elements. It is also possible for you to develop a wall composed of your own energy. The circle is extremely important in witchcraft as it can assist with energy and protection.

Remember that casting a circle does not have formal instructions for doing it correctly. You can use a wide range of tools for this purpose as you see fit. These include candles, crystals, flowers, twigs, herbs, and ropes. However, if you are still a beginner and looking for an idea to cast the circle and use it as your guide, here is a simple technique you can adhere to. You may modify it as you deem fit.

- Clear your sacred space from clutter - Ensure that there will be no source of disturbance as you cast the circle and perform your ritual afterward.
- Prepare four candles - Light them up, then arrange them based on the four cardinal directions - North (earth), South (fire), East (air), and West (water). The candle arrangement should have a diameter of five to six feet.
- After preparing all the tools you need, start centering yourself - The goal here is to let yourself be in a state of calm that is perfect for meditation. You know that you are ready when you have already achieved a superior state of calmness.
- Once ready, stand while facing the East - When in that position, call upon or summon the air spirits to give you guidance and protection. Do this for the remaining elements.
- Once done with all the elements, affirm by saying, *"I have cast the circle. Blessed be"* - Utilize this specific moment to start meditating or doing magic.

- After the ritual, dissolve the circle – Put off the candles and finish the entire practice with a gratitude heart meant specifically for the divine.

When casting a circle, remember there are no right and wrong steps. Similar to other similar practices, you must commit to applying your creativity and intuition in the practice. Make sure that you do whatever it is that you feel is right. Just don't forget to stick to the most important rule when casting the circle, which is the direction of the energy.

The Rule of Three (The Threefold Law)

Once you have successfully cast the circle, you can cast your spells or perform the intended ritual safely. When it is time for you to perform the magical ritual or work, you should never deviate from the ultimate Rule of Three, also called the Threefold Law or Law of Threefold Return.

This is an important rule/law in witchcraft as this requires you to follow the principle of avoiding the act of casting spells or performing rituals that aim to cause harm to someone or something. The reason is that if you do so, it will only activate bad karma, which is otherwise referred to by the witches as the Rule of Three.

This rule is a religious tenet that many Wiccans, occultists, and neo-pagans hold onto. Here, you will have to remind yourself all the time that whatever energy you release to the world, whether it is positive or negative, may go back to you threefold. Because of this principle, it is no longer surprising to see Wiccans describing this law as karma.

Based on some traditions, the threefold law or rule of three is not completely literal. However, it represents the fact that your energy will go your way again as many times as possible for you to learn and understand all the lessons linked to it. This is why you must be extra careful when performing rituals and crafting spells.

You have to be one hundred percent sure that it will never cause any harm to anyone, so you can avoid ruining yourself with your bad karma.

Chapter 5 – Protection and Defense Spells

You can't avoid stress and danger all the time. No matter how careful you are, there will still be several instances when you will feel stressed out and in danger. The problem is that any feeling of being unsafe or in danger, whether spiritually, physically, or emotionally, may sap your energy and cause your entire wellbeing to be overly strained.

Fortunately, you can now handle that feeling of being in danger with the aid of protection spells. These spells will be of great help whether you just want to improve your emotional wellbeing or your stability, no matter how stressful – and sometimes dangerous – the world is.

With the help of protection spells, you can give yourself a strong defense and protection from harm, stress, and bad energies and your family and your loved ones. The protection spells can also help you ward off toxic and unpleasant people, eliminate unhealthy influences, and protect everything that belongs to you.

Importance of Protection Spells

For the protection spell to affect change, you need to do it with a high level of focus and intent. Every time you craft spells and finally cast them, you serve as the agent whose goal is to activate change. You will be the one to direct and form energy to your preferred outcome. Since what you will be focusing on are the defense and protection spells and magic, expect them to work based on a certain set of intentions guaranteed to help in cleansing and getting rid of negativity.

Spells specifically meant to give you protection also have multiple facets. You can use them to protect someone or something from negative energy, defend yourself from an attack, and protect someone else or yourself from certain harm or danger. This type of spell is also important as it helps maintain a general defense level.

Protection spells are also important as they can make you feel personally and professionally protected. You can even use these spells as protection from possible harassment and bullying in the workplace. Anything that may cause permanent damage to your life can be dealt with by making protection spells and casting them at the right time.

The spells may also be useful in protecting your partner's integrity and keeping your relationship strong. This is possible as you can use the spells to avoid external forces that may interfere with your loving and secure relationship.

One more thing that protection spells can do is protect your wealth and health. You will no longer feel afraid when activating your protection shield through the spells, even when walking in harmful and dangerous situations.

You will feel at ease knowing you have a defense from anything and anyone that may harm or hurt you. The protection spells can give you a shielding layer that will encourage you to handle serious situations confidently.

As a guide to this type of spell, the first thing you will most likely have to do is cleanse your space as well as the tools you intend to use. Be clear on your intent, too. This means that you should clarify whatever you wish to achieve from the spell.

Visualizing your preferred outcome should come next. After that, you can do the exact steps for your ritual. End this process by expressing your gratitude.

Types of Protection Spells

Protection spells come in different forms and types. This means you can just pick one based on the kind and level of defense you would like to give yourself.

Basic Shield Protection

You can use this kind of protection spell anytime you feel like you need a basic shield or defense from harm. To do it, keep yourself centered first, then ground your energy. You can do the grounding if you take seven deep breaths. Imagine drawing up the energy from the Earth to your core as you take in each breath.

After that, visualize the energy as it extends past your core and expands as a means of creating a physical bubble surrounding you. You may look at the energy as something that resembles a soap bubble that slowly and gently encircles your whole body. If you want, you can expand the bubble even further if what you intend to encircle with the shield of protection is your whole apartment or house.

Secure the visualization by changing a protection spell – the one you crafted, preferably. The spell could be stated this way.

"I summon/invoke this shield of protection

Nothing can ail me or put me in danger while I am encircled in this magical protection."

Protection Charm

You can also create a protection charm that you can use to improve the results of your spells. It is okay to carry this charm with you all the time. You may use a piece of jewelry you already have at home and just add magic. Once enchanted, you can then wear the charm anytime and anywhere.

You may also want to buy a new jewelry piece specifically designed for protection. Let the jewelry pass through the smoke of incense to cleanse it first. You may also do the cleansing by doing a suitable ritual that you have chosen.

To use a protection charm for your spells, you must gather the following items.

- One incense stick – You may also use a bundle of smoke-cleansing herbs.
- Lighter or match
- A piece of jewelry

Here are the steps in taking advantage of this protection charm and spell.

- Cleanse your space. After that, you should define your intention. It should be clear enough to avoid confusion when trying to draw positive energy and drive negative ones away. Ground your energy right after.
- Use the lighter or match to light up the herb bundle or incense. Let the piece of jewelry pass through the smoke – after which, say this spell or another one with the same meaning as this one.

    "By the power carried by this purifying and cleansing smoke

    I am now cleansing you of every negative and unwanted energy."

- Hold the piece of jewelry using your hands. Imagine the earth's energy flowing up. Let it fill your core.
- Direct the flowing energy to the piece of jewelry, then say the following,

    "I am charging this item

    To serve as my shield, keeping me protected from danger and injury."

After that, the charm will be ready for use. Start wearing it anywhere you go to serve as your ultimate source of protection from harm.

Purifying Bath Protection Spell

This specific protection spell ritual is very beautiful and magical, as you can use it to cleanse not only your space but also your spirit. This type of spell anytime you feel like what you need is more than the usual quick fix. The good thing about the purifying bath is that it can help you relax deeply and make you feel comfortable.

Expect this ritual to focus on removing negative energies, so you can surround yourself with the protective shield. You may be able to find additional herbs and oils that you can use for this bath protection spell in your kitchen or pantry. Basically, though, the things you need for this spell are one cup of Epsom salt, three drops of sandalwood essential oil, and one teaspoon of dried rosemary.

- Mix the mentioned ingredients in a tiny bowl.
- Set an intention – The intention you can set could be in this line or anything similar, *"I am completely relaxed, comfortable, and protected."*

- Prepare the bath –Sstart sprinkling the Epsom salt blend beneath running water.
- Visualize the intention while letting yourself soak in the bath. Continue soaking for as long as possible – Once done, imagine every negative energy coming down together with the prepared bathwater.

One thing to note when creating this type of protection is that unlike all the other forms of spellwork, you should specifically focus on the protection's intent for rituals and spells. This should help you attain the best results.

Protective Amulets and Talismans

Talismans and amulets are built for certain purposes – one of which is protection. The two work together by immediately influencing the energy surrounding them, which is why you can see them being worn and carried frequently or positioned in an area's entryway or a central location.

A major difference is that a talisman focuses more on the signs and symbols used in creating it. You can choose certain protective symbols and allow them to work into the piece.

On the other hand, the amulet is mainly designed for your chosen and used materials. This means you can choose the items and materials for your spells and rituals and then direct their positive energies to the amulet by working them into the piece. Note, though, that you are allowed to combine the mentioned focuses. You can refer to the result as either a talisman, amulet, or just a charm, thereby covering each base.

Apart from protection, you can also use amulets and talismans for various purposes. You can create them to draw love, employment, or money. You can also make the talismans hold sigils or symbols that can help in attracting specific kinds of spiritual beings. You can use it mainly to protect yourself or perform other purposes.

To let you know about the protective symbols or sigils you can incorporate into your talismans, here is a list of some of them.

- Mars symbol – Generally, the energy emitted by Mars is protective, so you may want to use the symbol of this planet. You can use this as a sigil to protect you from possible accidents and stolen and lost damage, especially if you travel often.
- Pentagram – This one is also a generally protective symbol. You can use it to defend yourself from spiritual and psychic intrusion.

- Eye images and Hamsa - You can use this symbol to gain protection from the evil eye.
- Cross - It is a protective symbol for malignant spirits. It is ideal for you if you are following a suitable belief system.
- Janus image - It should protect locations, especially if you put it on the entryways.
- Crossed weapons - Any crossed weapons, like spears, symbolize the guardians who tend to block the way of those who are only looking for trouble.
- Eye of Horus - You will find this symbol useful when trying to protect yourself and your family from evil.
- Brigid's cross - This symbol is useful in keeping your home or any other property from fire and lighting.

Note that you can use bind runes and sigils to develop your protective symbols. Once you already have a protective amulet, talisman, or symbol, you can start bringing it with you anywhere or making it a part of your rituals and spells by ensuring that you also put it on the altar.

Casting a Circle of Protection

Probably the most effective and common form of protection ritual that you can use right now is the casting of the circle. As mentioned in the previous chapter, the circle is definitely one of the most valuable components of a ritual or spell. It is even more valuable when used for protection.

You may want to cast a circle of protection to ensure that you are fully protected whenever you perform magical work. When casting a protective circle, remember that you will need a space with a high level of energy. It should be a spot that will let you execute and perform magic safely without being interrupted by any harmful entity that may otherwise get attracted by the metaphysical energies that you possess during your spellcasting and rituals.

The first thing that you should do here is to mark out the circle. Make sure you are already fully aware of the exact spot where you can create the circle. Regardless of if you are doing the ritual or spell on an altar or any other part of your home or outdoors, pick a spot for the circle that will keep you undisturbed. That way, you can peacefully focus and work on your magic and ritual.

Use a long cord to mark the circle's boundaries. Alternatively, you can put some rocks or candles along all the edges. You can also use crystals that can provide additional protection to the circle.

Once marked, you can start conjuring pure energy capable of surrounding and protecting you. The good news is that there are several ways to do it, so you can rest assured that there is one that perfectly suits you as well as your practices.

Basic Circle of Protection

Casting this basic circle of protection is quick and easy as it does not involve using tools. Just follow the steps below.

- After marking out the circle, stand in the middle of it. Allow yourself to relax and practice deep breathing – Visualize your crown (top of the head) opening up like a funnel receiving the white and divine light. Note that the crown will always be connected to your higher self and the divine. This means that opening it up and amplifying this particular channel is possible based on your will.

- Open your arms – Your palms should also be facing out when doing this. As you take in each breath, imagine that you are pulling down the divine and pure light through the crown. Channel out the light every time you breathe out. You can do that through your palms. This should help in letting a protective shield surround you.

- Allow the high-vibration energy to fill the entire space surrounding you – When that happens, expect to experience a buzzing or tingling feeling. It may cause you to have goosebumps, or you may enjoy a light and uplifting feeling.

- Hold one outstretched arm – Point this arm to the circle's edge. Spin clockwise thrice, mentally allowing the divine light to mark out the circle. After that, lift both your arms over your head, then say something like this,

    "I summon the presence of the God and Goddess

    With your power and grace, bless this circle

    To keep me free, safe, and protected inside this sacred space

So mote it be."

Once you have said that, it indicates that you are already ready to perform the ritual or cast the spell. Close the circle properly upon the end of the ritual. Do that by holding your arm out and then spinning it around in an anti-clockwise motion thrice. You should then feel the dispersion of the protective and divine light. Do not forget to thank the spirits for being present before declaring the circle closed.

Advanced Circle of Protection

If you prefer to do a more advanced version of the circle of protection, then you can use this one as a guide. Here, you will need one compass and four candles. You may also want to use a wand or athame to direct energy. The candles could be white or colored and should represent each point or direction.

- North – green
- South – red
- East – yellow
- West – blue

Make use of the compass, then put each candle on every cardinal point. As you put and light each candle, say this one (make sure that you change the cardinal point and the represented element every time).

"Guardians of the (state the cardinal point or direction)

Element of the (state the represented element – earth for the north, air for the east, fire for the south, and water for the west)

I summon/invoke your presence during this ritual

Please be with me in my ritual and bless this circle."

Once you have finished lighting the candles in all cardinal points and directions, take your athame or wand. You should point this magical tool to the circle's edge. Spin around in a clockwise motion thrice.

After that, visualize a white and bright light penetrating your crown. Use either the athame or wand to direct such light out. It should be through your arm, then the tool, and then out. This should help in forming the circle's edge.

The next step is standing in the middle of the circle. Feel the white and divine light as it fills the circle and immerses your whole being. Say this during that stage.

"Guardian angels, spirit guides, and Gods and Goddesses
I summon/invoke your presence during this ritual
Grace this circle with your blessing, and help me stay protected
I forbid unwanted entities from entering this circle
Only divine and pure beings can enter my sacred space
I hereby cast the circle
So mote it be."

This should prompt your readiness to execute the ritual or cast your spell. After that, close the circle with the help of your athame or wand. Just spin this tool around in an anti-clockwise motion thrice, then feel and notice the dispersing of the protective light. Do not forget to thank the presence of elements and spirits. End this ritual by announcing the closing of the circle.

Chapter 6 – Magic Herbs and Plants

Plant magic is an old tradition that you can trace back to the ancient times of the Egyptians. When talking about plant magic, note that it involves using herbs and plants known for possessing magical powers and energies for a wide range of purposes - healing, protection, love spells, and self-empowerment.

Every plant or herb possesses magical properties, powers, and strengths, so you can use them to increase the power of your spells. If you use them, you can rest assured that you have a higher chance of attaining your desired results regardless of your level of strength as the crafter and caster of the spell.

The reason is that plants and herbs already contain many magical properties. The fact that plant magic has a lot of uses, not to mention being effective and having the ability to produce quick results, indicates its popularity among a lot of witchcraft practitioners until today.

How to Use Magic Herbs and Plants?

With the proven powers and magical properties of herbs and plants, you will notice that they are not only used by witches for healing. You can also see these plants being used in alternative medicines, as well as in food and health supplements and dietary products.

When it comes to using them for your spells, though, the best method would be sprinkling some herbs into a candle flame while performing your ritual. By doing that, you can make your spells more powerful.

You can also find other ways to make plants and herbs a part of your spell work and rituals. The good news is that most of these methods are easy and quick to do.

- Mix them and visualize their results and effects – This is an effective tip when it comes to making herbs a part of your spell. By doing this, you can pass on the magical properties, powers, and energies of the herbs to your spell. This can make your spell stronger and more vigorous.
- Roll anointed or oiled candles into your chosen herb or herb mixture – This simple technique works in transmitting the energies of the herbs to the anointed or oiled candles. The energies and powers transmitted to the candles will also be spread to their flame and your spell or ritual.
- Burn your chosen herbs – Burning them in small discs or charcoal blocks is highly recommended.
- Put the herbs of your choice in an incense burner tray made of metal – After that, light the herbs and burn them.
- Burn every sturdy herb you can think of directly – Some examples of these herbs are mugwort, cedar, and sage. These are flammable herbs that it is possible to light them on fire directly.
- Set them on fire – This method is necessary for cleansing. With that said, you can do it in any part of performing the spell. It could be before, during, and after the spell. The magical plants and herbs can help clear away negative energies, thereby preparing you for the spell or ritual. It can also help in getting rid of negative energies brought by the spell to the surface.
- Create potions – You can also use herbs and plants to make magical potions. Once you have these potions, you can start using them in your spells and rituals.
- Create tinctures, oils, herb bags, and incenses – Having these items made of magical herbs and plants around can help you work on your spell or ritual for a long time, usually for a few months at a time. As each spell works, you can also expect the

herbal product or essence to add or integrate more energy into it.

When it comes to using magic plants and herbs for your rituals and spells, you should remind yourself that even just a little amount of them can already work wonders. They are so powerful, so even if you start small, you can already get good results. Just add more herbs if necessary. Also, you should never ingest the herbs and plants used for your spells and rituals. The reason is that doing so can only put you in danger.

Another way to take advantage of the magic herbs and plants is to leave a small amount of them in all parts of your home. This should help in getting rid of negative energies surrounding your home and offering you protection. It can also bring happiness and peaceful energy while promoting good health.

Another common practice is carrying a charm bag containing various magical herbs. Bring this charm bag with you all the time so you can enjoy a lot of positive things from it, including love and protection. It is also advisable to do plant magic or gather magical herbs and plants at night. It should preferably be under a full moon as this is the time when they are most powerful.

Herbs and Plants for Spellcrafting and Spellcasting

Now, let's familiarize ourselves with the long list of herbs and plants known for holding a lot of healing and magical properties. With the properties they hold, you have an assurance that they can help raise and enhance the energy of your ritual and spellwork.

Acacia

Also called mimosa, Arabic gum, or wattle, acacia has magick properties that can provide protection against the "evil eye." Bless (or asperge) your candles, censers, and other tools with it; you can also anoint/bless containers holding your magick tools. In addition to aiding in meditation, you can use it in your bathing ritual to ward off bad spells or keep future issues at bay.

Aloe

This fantastic plant is so powerful that it can provide you with not only protection but also luck and fortune. Place it on your loved ones' resting place for peace, or use it in your home to promote luck and protection for those living under your roof.

Want a new lover in your life? Burn aloe at night (and particularly on a full moon), and you can bring a new lover into your life. Some use it to have a former lover return to the nest! In addition to its great uses in the field of magic and witchcraft, this plant is also capable of easing several skin problems.

Amber

This plant is recognized for its ability to protect against many forms of danger, whether it is psychic attacks from within or evil spells/attacks from outside sources. It can promote a high level of focus and mental clarity. It even works in turning negative energies into positive ones. Just avoid consuming the berries of this plant because they are toxic.

Angelica

Powerful protection against many forms of negative energy! Like acacia, sprinkle it around your home, and place it in your bath water. You can add it to your incense burner to help with healing. Again, like the acacia, it's a powerful sort of protection from hexes.

Anise

Similar to Angelica above. Protect yourself from the evil eye. But wait, there's more! This wonderful herb helps with digestion issues as well. After meals, consider drinking star anise tea for help with gas, bloating, and constipation. Also, include it in your spells, use it in incense, and even slip it into your pillowcase to help ward off bad dreams.

Basil

OK, this one is a bit different. Needing more abundance in terms of money? Add hot water to a batch of these powerful leaves, and get to mopping! Need that job? Go sprinkle basil leaves around the bottom of the office building in which you want a job. Or use it around your business structure to attract capital and bring success.

Some wear basil in a necklace/charm/amulet to bring money and prosperity.

Bergamot

Nature's SSRI (antidepressant). Instead of drugs, try this to improve your memory and your sleep! It is also called "Orange Mint."

Black Pepper

Use black pepper before cleansing yourself or your sacred space through smudging or incense. What you should do is burn it so you can eliminate bad, negative, and toxic energies from your household.

You may also want to carry black peppercorns around. This helps banish the evil eye and any feeling of jealousy. Mix black pepper with salt, then scatter this mixture around your home. This should secure your property from any bad and evil energy.

Buckwheat

Buckwheat is also a great partner in your spells and charms. Like many others in this list, use it to attract riches. Need to balance your budget? Put a bowl of buckwheat flour and dried peas somewhere inside your home; don't forget to throw it out once you've reached your goals.

Caraway

The caraway plant has a strong connection to so many positive aspects of life! Use it to bless your ritual tools and protect your home from evil spirits. Some even put this powerful herb under their baby's cradle. Use this plant to bring you good health, increased mental abilities, soaring passion, and loving protection,

You can also use it together with other similar herbs and plants, such as the roots of Angelica.

Cinquefoil

Many consider the cinquefoil a magical one-size-fits-all! Its five-petal ends are representative of five important parts of life: love, power, health, wisdom, and money. You can, therefore, use this herb for a variety of purposes – one of which would be cleansing and blessing your house for protection against bad omens.

You can also create an herb infusion using cinquefoil. Once you have the infusion, wash your forehead and arms with it nine times. This should help in washing out and banishing evil spells and hexes made against you.

Another way to take advantage of the power of this herb is to get an empty eggshell and then fill it up with the cinquefoil. You should then keep it in your home so you can receive protection against evil forces.

Finally, some use red flannel cloth to wrap it up and hang it over sleeping quarters as a way to protect from evil spirits.

Dragon's Blood

Want/need to banish and fight off bad habits or negative influences? Grind Dragon's Blood and sprinkle it around your home to keep you protected from such things.

Eucalyptus

Eucalyptus is also a great magical herb, as it is capable of attracting healing vibrations. It also works incredibly well as far as healing and protection are concerned. Burn eucalyptus, so you can purify your space. You should also carry it with you in the form of an amulet or sachet. Doing this helps in reconciling any difficulty you have with your relationships.

Horehound

How about some mental clarity and enhanced creativity during your spellwork? Horehound also carries properties that promote balance in your personal energy and is perfect for use when you are clearing or blessing your home. Keeping it near doorways is also believed to keep trouble at bay.

Gardenia

Like many other herbs/plants, gardenia is great for warding away evil, strife – and for protecting one's home from such negative outside enemies. Need some peace? Incorporate it into your flower arrangements, incenses, and other healing mixtures.

Garlic

Lots of magical uses for this popular plant. You've surely read stories where it was used in exorcism or to fight off vampires! The lesson here is that this smelly (yet oft-used component of Italian food) has a lot of uses, serving as an effective defense against negative magic, the envy of others, and any sort of spiritual darkness.

Marshmallow Root

It is also a great idea to include a marshmallow root in your spells and rituals. Burning it as incense can promote a higher level of psychic stimulation and protection. You may also want to put a marshmallow root on the altar when performing a ritual. This can help in drawing in and inviting good spirits.

Myrrh

Let's talk about vibrational or spiritual energy; it's the basis for creating change in your life. Myrrh carries a strong connection with vehicles used in reaching such heightened states and also promotes alignment. Use it in incense, add it to charms, or burn it with Frankincense. Yes, just like the Christmas story: the Wise Men brought Frankincense and Myrrh as gifts to baby Jesus.

Quince

Looking for Love? Happiness? Better luck? A "bodyguard" for evil? Look no further! Put some of these powerful seeds in a red flannel bag and say goodbye to physical attacks and harmful circumstances. Use it in your spells and charms to enhance its powers!

St. John's Wort

You can wear this herb as a means of preventing fever and colds. It also works for those who are looking for a sort of protection from black witchcraft. Just put this herb in a jar, then place it in one of your windows. You may also burn St. John's Wort in your fireplace to encourage protection from evil spirits, fire, and lightning.

This chapter covers just a few of the hundreds of magical herbs and plants that you can use to increase the power and potency of your spells. Make them a part of your spells and rituals, and you will surely enjoy their healing properties and get the results you want from your spellwork.

Chapter 7 – Candle Magick Spells

Candles usually have mystical meanings aside from their primary function of providing light. As a matter of fact, candles have been used as primary elements in several magical practices and spells, including Wicca and Pagans. Several magic practitioners also have their individual perspectives and concepts regarding candles.

Generally, candle magic is a simple form of spellcasting. It is simple in that it does not require plenty of fancy ceremonial and ritual tools. This means that even if you only have a candle, you can already cast a spell.

Utilized in spellwork for over 25,000 years, the use of candles is a pure form of sympathetic magic. You can see these candles being widely used in rituals as a means of representing not only people but also things, influences, and emotions.

As the one who casts a spell, you should focus your intent on influencing your preferred outcome as indicated by the candle. If you intend to use candles to represent another person when performing sympathetic magic, make sure that you ask for permission first.

Almost every witch and magic practitioner use candles in their practice regardless of their magical tradition or belief system. Not everyone likes to use candles, though. However, as you continue practicing spellcrafting and witchcraft, you will realize their widespread use eventually.

Candles represent life as well as the spirit that tends to come to life through the fire element, home symbol, and burning in the hearth. With its connection to the fire element, you can focus your intention and energy on the burning candle, making it possible for you to manifest your goal and make it happen into reality.

For you to start candle magic, continue reading this chapter so you will know the actual steps on how to perform this form of witchcraft.

Setting Goals in Candle Magic

Setting your goal is an important first step in candle magic. This means that before you light a candle or cast a candle spell, you have to be fully aware of the exact reasons for performing such a ritual. In other words, you need to have already established an intention for your ritual and spellwork.

Note that candle magic can have a wide range of purposes. For one, you can use it to protect not only yourself but also others. It also serves as an instrument for attaining your goal in life and as an aid when performing your meditation. Moreover, you can perform candle magic so you will receive enough guidance for your everyday life.

Note, though, that if you petition for something, you can't expect the candle to work on its own. The result will still depend on you, your goal or petition, and how you perform it. This makes clearly defining your goal extremely important. You need a clear definition of whether the intention for this magical work using candles is for yourself or someone else.

If you wish to cast a spell on someone, make sure that you ask for permission. If you don't, then you will be at risk of performing candle magic against their will. This may cause you to break such an important rule that witchcraft practitioners should follow.

Selecting the Right Candle

In candle magic, you can't just use any candle without determining if it is the most appropriate or suitable one for you. Pick a candle that best suits you and your needs. It should fit your spell's intention or wish. In this case, you have to learn about the symbols associated with each candle color. In the absence of a colored candle, go for a white one. Just make sure that it also fits your goal or intention. You may use table, taper, and tealight candles when casting your spells.

Another important reminder is that the candle's size will have a major impact on how long the ritual will last. You can also find some practitioners who use engraved, pyramidal, and square-shaped candles in their spells and rituals. Note, though, that regardless of the shape and external appearance of the candle, they will still have the same level of effectiveness, provided you use the right one for the correct spell.

Also, you have to charge the candles with a certain intention. To make that happen, carve your goal or petition on the candle or anoint it to embody your exact intention.

What Does Every Candle Color Mean?

In relation to the previous section, which is all about selecting the right candle, you need to get to know the individual meanings of each candle color. That way, you will be able to select one that fits the specific intention and goal you have in mind.

Also, to create unique spells, you have to make your associations. Each candle color must connect to you personally. It should talk to you deeply, so you can make the most out of including it in your spells and rituals.

White Candle

This candle represents purity. It is vital in all fertility rituals. It is the most commonly used as white candles can improve and favor any kind of spell provided it comes with a good and positive purpose. That said, it is no longer surprising to see many practitioners referring to the white candle as the most versatile. You can use it for all types of rituals, spellcasting work, and meditation.

Black Candle

This one is a prominent symbol of protection and power. It perfectly suits protection magic, particularly spells meant to seek the help of the gods as well as your loved ones. The color black also works in fostering the evolution and development of your wisdom as well as that of the gods.

Red Candle

The color red, when applied in candle magic, strongly represents passion. With that said, it is the main color used by those who would like to perform love spells. For instance, you can use the red candle if you want to hold a ritual with the goal of finding a new lover or bringing back an ex.

It is also useful in making love potions. Basically, anything that revolves around love and romance can be associated with the red candle. You can even connect it to virility and sexuality.

Purple Candle

You can also use the color purple in candle magic. A purple candle is what you need if you intend to invoke spiritual energy. If your ritual aims to communicate with spirits, the afterlife, the deceased, or angels, then you need to light a purple candle on your altar.

Yellow Candle

In candle magic, yellow means wealth. You can relate a candle with a yellow color to any material position, such as jewels and money. You can greatly benefit from performing a spell or ritual that uses a yellow candle if you have labor relations or trade deals.

Pink Candle

A pink candle is a symbol of self-love. It is strongly connected to vanity and honor, which is also why it closely touches the world of femininity. The pink candle also aims to help in fighting violence. It is useful every time you need to create and cast a spell designed to sweeten and soften an aggressive and violent personality.

Blue Candle

If you are looking for a candle that you can use in your rituals that is a symbol of health, go for one in blue. You can significantly increase the effects of your physical healing spells and any other magical work relevant to diseases and medicine if you use the blue candle.

Green Candle

This candle is a symbol of the material world. It encompasses even the simplest forms of nature as well as the most complicated beings. It also includes all the things that live in a similar plane as other living things. You can use this green candle when performing ritual magic and spells that need a significant amount of hope.

Brown Candle

The brown candle represents the earth. It is a symbol of ancient magic that has a close relationship to the fields, fruits, and crops since people committed to agriculture are the ones who perform it. The good thing about the brown candle is that it tends to increase its strength during autumn as the first leaves fall.

Orange Candle

The orange candle is meant to represent the sun. It encompasses a lot of different fields, including calmness and peace, as well as the need to counter bad financial situations. Many of those who practice magic and witchcraft also relate the orange candle to one's ability to assimilate knowledge and concentrate.

Preparing the Altar

Once you have chosen your candle, you should start preparing the altar. Look for the most suitable area where you can practice candle magic. Note that it does not have to be anything fancy. You can just look for any room or area in your home that gives you a chance to be alone.

It should give you enough privacy and peace and should not have any form of interruption. Once you have chosen your sacred space, you can set up your altar using everything you need for your rituals/spells, including the appropriate candle.

Dressing the Candles

For your candle magic to work and produce the most favorable results, purify and consecrate the candles prior to using them in your rituals and spells. This means you should anoint them so you can charge them with your willpower and appropriate intentions. This particular step in candle magic also helps in eliminating every residual energy that comes from the source of your candle.

Note, though, that it is not a complete requirement to dress your candle before every spell. It will be a personal decision. You can decide to dress it if you wish to integrate some more power and intent into the spell.

- Pick a suitable oil – This should serve as the first step in dressing up the candle you intend to use for your spell and ritual. Choose an oil depending on the exact kind of ritual you wish to do as well as your intentions.

- Use one of your hands to hold the candle – Wet the middle and index fingers of your other hand using the oil.

- After that, rub the oil over the whole candle – Do it in such a way that you do not touch the wick. You have the option to begin from the bottom and work up or from the top, then go down.

- While rubbing the oil over the candle, visualize your intention – Imagine how it will manifest, too. Spend one to two minutes focusing on this particular step.

After that, it is safe to say that you have successfully dressed the candle.

Casting the Spell

The next parts of this chapter will tackle just a few examples of spells that use colored candles. You already know the individual meanings of the different colors of candles used in candle magic, so it is time to learn about some spells that you can cast using some of the mentioned colors.

White Candle for Spirit and House Cleansing Spell

You can cast this spell either on someone to cleanse his/her aura or your home to get rid of or banish negative energies. For you to perform this spell, you need to prepare one each of palo santo and sage stick, one white candle, and one large ashtray or a cauldron.

- Prepare your altar – You can do that by putting the candle next to the ashtray or cauldron.
- Light the palo santo stick – Once it begins burning, put it inside the ashtray or cauldron.
- Light the sage bundle next – Put it inside the ashtray or cauldron, too.
- While the smoke rises, light the candle, then chant this prayer,

    "Earth Goddess and the Celestial Dome

    Purify my heart

    Clear my home from negativity."
- Sing or whisper the chant – You can choose how you wish to deliver the chant, but your goal should be to invite benevolent energies capable of protecting your home.
- Continue chanting as many times as possible – Light the sticks again if necessary and allow their smoke to continue filling the room.
- Meditate – Once you are ready, you can finally blow out the candle. You may also choose to let the light of the candle go naturally but never leave it unattended.

Black Candle for Protection Against a Curse Spell

The black candle is so powerful that you can use it to protect yourself, even against a curse or work of witchcraft created by your evil enemy. It is what this spell is going to focus on. It is a straightforward protection spell that can fight against a curse or any other evil work cast on you.

To make this spell work, perform it for three consecutive days using three new candles every time. Ensure that they look the same. Once you have completed the three days, throw all waste you used for this spell in the trash.

Also, if you are unsure of the name of the enemy who cast an evil work on you, you are allowed to use the word "enemy." Do the spell at night during a full moon after 8 pm.

To perform this spell, gather the following items.

- 3 black candles
- Salt
- Matches
- Knife or athame
- Disposable plate
- Pepper powder

Here is also how you can do this black candle protection spell.

- Begin this spell with one black candle – If you know the name of your enemy, write it on this candle. When writing, begin at the bottom part of the candle.
- Get the salt and plate – Form a circle using salt in the plate. With your knife or athame, cut the candle at the bottom. This should let you see a second wick.
- Sprinkle the pepper over the whole candle – Light it while saying the following,

    "The light of this candle I offer to light

    To undo and turn back every sorcery, witchcraft, intrigue, gossip, envy, and evil made against (state your name) by (state the name of your enemy) at this exact time and moment

    So be it."
- Let the candle burn on the disposable plate until fully consumed – Just continue keeping an eye on it to prevent it from causing a fire.

Red Candle Love Spell

This is a love spell that uses a red candle, which can help you in making someone want you. You can cast it on someone whom you want to fall for you. Upon manifesting, expect this love spell to draw that person to your life. To perform this love spell, you need one red candle, one needle, one green thread, seven coins, and two large leaves you can draw.

- Get the candle and inscribe your full name, including your first and last name, in it - Inscribe the complete name of the one whom you want to attract.
- In one of the leaves, draw a picture of yourself - You should also use the other leaf to draw a picture of your love.
- Use the green thread and needle to sew the two leaves together - Tie them into a knot.
- Light the red candle. Chant the following:

  "Earth, air, fire, and water, listen to my prayer

  Bring me to (state the name of the person) who I love and desire genuinely

  I am ending this ritual without causing harm to anyone."
- Look for a crack in a tree and put the leaves in there.
- Get the seven coins and bury them around the tree, too.

Purple Candle Spell to Relieve Anxiety

As the name suggests, the goal of this spell is to banish your anxiety. It also aims to improve your confidence. The good news is that you do not need a lot of things to cast this spell. You only need one purple candle as well as your clear intentions.

- Light the purple candle.
- Take three deep cleansing breaths - Allow yourself to inhale positivity, calmness, and peace. Exhale negativity, stress, and anxiety.
- Look at the flame emitted by the candle while reciting this.

  "Anxious thoughts and racing mind

  I am setting an intention for all of you to stop

  Doubts and feelings abound

  Positive energies shut you down

Pride within while holding my head high
Anxiety can't win as I cast this spell
Clarity of mind and gratefulness, I can attain
So mote it be."

- Chant this as many times as possible – Just make sure to take three deep cleansing breaths every time you chant or recite it.
- Once you have completed the spell, you can choose to snuff out the candle or wait for it to burn down completely. Dispose of all the remains of your spell while ensuring that you do not forget to express your gratitude.

With these few examples of spells and rituals that require the use of candles, you now have some sort of idea of how you can perform candle magic and ensure that you get favorable and desirable results from it.

Chapter 8 – Seasonal Spells for Sabbats

Sabbats refer to the holidays that all witches and other practitioners of witchcraft worldwide celebrate. Those are the days that serve as the pillars of what we refer to as the circle of life, an unending cycle of nature. You can see it being represented by the sabbats surrounding the wheel of the year.

Wheel of the Year Defined

The wheel of the year that we are talking about in this chapter refers to a certain kind of calendar split into 8 parts or sections. Note that the sabbats work by dividing the entire year into 8 equal sections or parts. They are the ones that mark the start of every season and the mid-points. Each sabbat also falls into any of its two major categories.

- **Lesser Sabbats** - Also called the sun sabbats, the lesser sabbats consist of Yule, Litha, Mabon, and Ostara. These are holidays representing the start of every season. They are also more popularly known as equinoxes and solstices.
- **Greater Sabbats** - These consist of moon sabbats and earth festivals, including the Beltane, Imbolc, Samhain, and Lammas. Such holidays mark the middle point of every season. Expect each sabbat to fall on a certain day, which makes them different from the other four sabbats, which tend to shift based on the

year.

The mentioned sabbats were derived from the pagan traditions in Western Europe. Basically, the sabbats are days of festivities and celebrations designed to give honor and respect to not only the Gods but also to the earth and humans.

Note, though, that contrary to the claims of modern-day Wiccans, you can't find any evidence that shows the presence of the wheel of the year in modern or present form. However, there is clear proof that the Celts, who were around thousands of years ago, had celebrations for the festivals highlighted by the wheel.

Ancient Celtic culture also indicated how time was perceived as cyclical. This means that even if seasons change, you can't find anything that's lost since everything tend to go back following a repetitive natural cycle. While the modern world often regards time as linear nowadays, many still continuously recognize life's cyclical nature.

The Eight Sabbats

As mentioned a while ago, sabbats refer to the eight festivals that neopagans and Wiccans celebrate every year. These festivals are spaced in even intervals throughout the entire annual cycle of the season of the earth (wheel of the year). Let's get to know more about these eight sabbats and how you can celebrate each one and perform seasonal spells in this chapter.

Yule (Dec. 12 to Jan. 1)

Often falling around or on the 21st of December, Yule occurs on the winter solstice. Yule holds the longest night and the shortest day every year. Note, though, that even if the long night may feel like the world is plunging into darkness, most witches still consider it a time of happiness and joy. The reason is that it serves as the starting point for the reentry of light into the world.

Once the winter solstice is over, you can expect the year's darkest part to end. This will cause the days to start becoming longer. In the all-embracing myth of the neo-Pagans, Yule is also the day of birth of the divine infant conceived during the spring. Certain beliefs state that Yule is the exact time of the year that represents the rebirth of the sun god. The rebirth is meant to bring back the light to you.

The Yule is also one of the coldest moments of the year, which prompts action to further lead into reflection. This means that Yule is a moment of thought and reflection. With that in mind, you may want to spend time reminiscing what happened last year.

You may also honor lost loved ones and family members during the Yule. This way, you can give them a place where they can participate in the festivities even if they have departed from the world of the living.

How to Celebrate Yule?

If you are just starting your journey towards understanding Yule, one thing that you can do is burn the yule log. It is a tradition that began in medieval times. You have to light up the log to encourage the return of the sun.

Look for a Yule log on your own outside. Decorate it using herbs, string, or any other item you can burn for the spell. If you can't access a pit or fireplace, then you can use inset candles. You can also perform a sunrise ritual.

- Look for a spot outdoors or inside your home where you can see the sun rising or coming up.
- Prepare a chalice containing orange juice – This item should have been blessed already. Once the sun rises, toast the return of the god.
- Recite chants, prayers, or incantations for the lord – These chants and prayers may also be to encourage hope for the coming new year. In case you need something, you may also set your intention for this ritual. You can then send out your heartfelt and genuine prayers to the universe.
- Drink from the chalice – However, leave some so you can bring it outside and then pour it into the earth. This should serve as your offering to the god.

Apart from this ritual, you can also do spellwork during this sabbat that revolves around happiness, hope, peace, love, and strengthening bonds.

Imbolc (Feb. 1 to 2)

Imbolc is a sabbat that falls on the 2nd of February. It marks the middle point of the winter. Imbolc is a word that means "in the belly." It represents the time when the sheep usually get pregnant. Such a concept was woven into the entire sabbat as a moment of fertility, hope, and rebirth.

Celebrations during this specific time of the year often include making a sun wheel and then burning it, which is a symbol of life's continuity. This sabbat also serves as the ideal time for you to do spring cleaning. You can use this moment to get rid of clutter and begin fresh. The energy emitted by Imbolc also signifies the need to rejuvenate everything.

Apart from cleansing physical clutter, you can also use this time to clear your mind. It provides the right energy to release the old, allowing you to encourage the entry of the new. This is a good thing as it also provides room for the coming of new opportunities.

How to Celebrate Imbolc?

One tradition that will allow you to celebrate and honor this particular sabbat is to leave out some food and drink during the Imbolc eve. This could be buttered bread, seeds, grains, or milk.

Put buttered bread in one bowl, too. Leave it indoors for the traveling fairies and Lady of Greenwood. Make sure to dispose of everything the next day as they no longer have existing essence by that time.

You may also want to perform a ritual specifically designed for the returning light. What's good about this ritual is that it is simple, plus you can let the other members of your family, including children, participate.

- Start by making the participants of this ritual, including children, turn out each light in your home after dark - Light a pillar candle or votive only.
- Provide a small candle, like a chime candle or tealight, for every participant - Once it is already dark, let every participant light the candle they are holding from the larger one.
- Discuss the connection of Imbolc to fire and Brigid, a goddess - You may also talk about the fact that the candle's light symbolizes the warmth and light of the upcoming spring. Do this, especially if some of your participants include kids.
- Reflect on the meaning of darkness - You also have to reflect on the way it is a beginning and end, as well as the birth and death of a cycle. Express your gratitude or thanks to the darkness while inviting the returning light.
- End the ritual by making every participant make a wish before they blow out their own candles.

When it comes to spells, the ones that are ideal during the Imbolc sabbat are those for blessings, fertility, cleansing, wishing, protection, and luck.

Ostara (Mar. 19 to 21)

Ostara is an equinox that signifies that it is the right time to attain the perfect balance between darkness and light. The name was derived from Eostre, a goddess. This sabbat is also the perfect time for fertility. This means that it represents abundance and fertility, as proven by the sabbat's two primary symbols – the hare and the eggs.

When Ostara comes, expect day and night to be of equal length. It is a cycle that still belongs to the waxing phase. Starting from this point, the days will start becoming longer compared to nights.

Apart from being the time for new life and fertility, Ostara is also meant for harmony and balance. With that said, it is the ideal moment for you to balance yourself as well as the subtle energies that are inside of you, including your chakras, your inner feminine and masculine traits, and your dark and light aspects, among others.

When this sabbat comes, observe agricultural changes, like the sudden warming of the ground, closely. Wait for the plants to surface from the ground slowly but surely.

How to Celebrate Ostara?

One way to celebrate Ostara is to plant anything. As a spring equinox, it is the ideal moment for planting seeds in your garden. You are also allowed to perform a simple seed spell using an indoor plant.

- Pick a seed you wish to grow – During the selection, make it a point to think of an intention that you also wish to plant and cultivate into your own life.
- Plant the seed in a pot – Keep your intention in mind while doing so. If you want, you may chant or keep on repeating a mantra.
- Nurture the plant – After planting it during the Ostara, make it a point to nurture it by providing it with sufficient sunlight and water. Nurture your intention, too. You can do that by taking even just small steps as a means of reaching your goal. Expect your intention to also turn into a reality as you witness the plant growing.

You may also cast some spells that are appropriate for the Ostara. Some of the spells that are good to cast during this sabbat are those meant for fertility, finding balance, starting fresh, new beginnings, motivation and creativity, rebirth and renewal, and love and connections.

Beltane (Apr. 30 to May 1)

Taking place around the 1st day of May, Beltane is a sabbat that is halfway in between Litha (the summer solstice) and Ostara (the spring equinox). It is the midpoint between summer and spring. One important fact about Beltane is that it is a joyful moment representing the union and marriage of God and Goddess.

Beltane is also the period of fertility. Many believe that it is the most fertile and sexually charged moment of the year, as you can see in the blooming greenery and the beginning of the cycle of planting.

How to Celebrate Beltane?

Take a walk around nature, then collect some branches and flowers. Use them in decorating your altar. If possible, use seasonal flowers to fill it up, like birch trees and hawthorn, which are considered extremely significant during this time of the year. It is also advisable to put some green ribbons and cloth on your altar.

Moreover, you should make it a point to light green and red candles as both represent growth and love. It is also the perfect time to burn floral or earthy incense in your sacred space.

Handfasting is another beautiful ceremony that you can do when the Beltane sabbat comes. This involves two people who will have to hold hands while in a standing position. One more person uses a red ribbon to wrap the two of them.

What's good about this ceremony is that it represents how committed two people are toward each other. Even after removing the ribbon, the handfasting ceremony performed during Beltane will remind them that they still have the commitment to stay together even without tying their hands.

With the concept behind handfasting, it is no longer surprising to see it being performed by romantic couples. It is also possible to do it with friends, parents, and children, as well as any two people willing to show their love and commitment to each other.

Litha (Jun. 20 to 22)

Litha is a celebration of the year's longest day at the summer solstice. Many perceive this sabbat as full of light. It is the right time for you to go after fun and work, as you will notice the day lengthening. However, do not forget that it also serves as a mark that the days that grow longer are on their way to an end.

Litha is also a commemoration of the day when the Oak King gives back his power to Holly King, his twin brother, intending to continue nature's cycle. Bonfire, which represents how strong the sun is during this time, is a major part of this sabbat.

Note that Litha is also a moment of celebration and joy. You can look at all your achievements in the first six months of the year when you celebrate Litha. You can then revel in the warmth and light offered by the sun, as after this point, you will receive the moon's power.

How to Celebrate Litha?

Of course, the ultimate way to celebrate Litha is to host a bonfire since this sabbat revolves around the sun's fiery aspect. You can, therefore, celebrate fertility by setting up a roaring and blazing fire in your backyard. If you want, you can host this bonfire for your loved ones.

You may want to light sparklers after dark, too. Do not forget to provide offerings to your traditional gods. When setting up a bonfire, though, you need to adhere to the basic safety rules. This is to prevent hurting someone when celebrating this sabbat.

Litha is also the right moment for doing spell workings associated with health, happiness, love, relationships, luck, and protection. Another way to take advantage of Litha is to create your energy bag. You can make such a bag using the steps below.

- Collect some herbs, crystals, or any other object linked to life and vibrancy.
- Get a small drawstring bag, then fill it up with the items you collected.
- Leave out this bag under the sun – This should prompt it to collect energy that you can use in your rituals and spells later.

Note that Litha has the most energy derived from sunlight the entire year. However, you can't expect the bag you created to hold such energy indefinitely. That said, you should make it a point to recharge it by exposing it to sunlight regularly.

Lammas/Lughnasadh (Aug. 1 to 2)

Lammas is a celebration of the first harvest, which is also otherwise referred to as the grain harvest. It happens during the height of summer when you can see the fields and greens being filled with crops and flowers. It shows that the harvest is coming near.

Lammas is indeed a great moment to relax while reflecting on the coming abundance that the fall months will bring. It is also during Lammas when you should reap what you sow during the past months.

This sabbat focuses not only on the aspect of early harvest but also on celebrating Lugh, a Celtic god. It is a festival meant to recollect and celebrate everything that you have gathered and worked through the entire year. It, therefore, also shows true gratitude.

Lammas is an incredible opportunity to create a list of all the things you learned, achieved, and experienced this year. This will open up your eyes to the many things that you are thankful for.

How to Celebrate Lammas?

The best way to commemorate this special festival is to take the time to decorate your altar, home, or sacred space. Decorate it in such a way that it signifies the colors of nature as well as abundance – the ones that you are celebrating in Lammas. Among the decorations you can add to your sacred space, altar, or home that will surely add magic to the season are the following:

- In-season flowers – Some examples are sunflowers, coneflowers, snapdragons, and zinnia
- Herb clippings taken from your garden
- A bowl containing in-season fruits and vegetables
- Candles that are in the colors of red, yellow, orange, and green – If you don't have colored ones, use natural beeswax candles.
- Crystals known for supporting the season – These include pyrite, tiger's eye, citrine, carnelian, and green aventurine.
- Any grain-like sheaves of corn husks and wheat

Preparing for a Lammas feast is also a great way to celebrate this season. The feast should consist of every local ingredient you can think of. Ensure that you use grains in your feast, too. This should honor the season's abundance.

Decorate the table you will be using for the feast with fresh flowers or any of the items we mentioned a while ago for decorating your sacred space. Feast with your loved ones to rejoice in the beauty of the first harvest and the abundant nature.

Mabon (Sep. 21 to 24)

Mabon is the season that commemorates the 2nd harvest of the year. Basically, it is all about the harvest of fruits and veggies. It is ideal to hold a great feast during this specific season to demonstrate your gratitude for every blessing you received the entire year.

This is also the sabbat, which serves as the perfect moment for reflecting and looking back on the plans and hopes you had at the start of the year. That way, you will get an idea of your progress.

Moreover, Mabon is a season that holds the balance between darkness and light. This means that both day and night have equal lengths. You will enjoy a sense of harmony and balance coinciding with the sun as it moves to Libra, a sign symbolized by the scales.

How to Celebrate Mabon?

You can celebrate Mabon through meditation. For this purpose, you may want to decorate a special altar specifically made for you to meditate during this season. You can arrange apples, baby gourds, sheaves of grains, or pumpkins in this space. Include yellow, light orange, or brown candles, too.

- Begin by sitting in front of your meditation altar. Look closely at every item you arranged on the altar. Allow them to bring out safe and calm emotions.
- With your eyes closed, start noticing your breathing patterns. Breathe in for 4 counts, then out for 5 counts. Do this until you start calming down your thoughts. Do not worry if you still have other thoughts. Just continue bringing your attention to and focusing on your breath.
- Sit in that calm position for around 10 to 20 minutes. Feel the peace and safety infusing you in the form of bright and healing light. If you have a mantra, like the one below, you can say and repeat it during this time.

"Everything I need, I own

The abundance of nature and the universe will take care of me."

Expect this meditation practice performed in time for the celebration of Mabon to make you feel good and content with the abundance that nature and the universe can provide you.

Samhain (Oct. 31 to Nov. 1)

Samhain is a sabbat that falls on the 31st day of October, which is also the actual date of Halloween. It is in this sabbat wherein you will notice the veil separating the worlds to be at the thinnest. With that in mind, it is definitely the perfect time to honor everything that you have lost. This sabbat also marks the year's final harvest, which is mostly an abundant harvest of berries and nuts, as you prepare for the winter.

When holding a feast for this sabbat, setting an extra spot for your ancestors and departed loved ones is common. It is the time when you talk about them, offer them food, and honor their memory. It is because the Samhain is the time wherein you can let them join you in the festivities.

Samhain is also recognized as the new year of most witchcraft practitioners and witches. It is the renewal of the wheel of the year's cycle. That said, it is also the perfect moment for reflection. Reflect and release everything that happened throughout the year so you can finally prepare yourself for a new season.

How to Celebrate Samhain?

When it comes to celebrating Samhain, you should remember that the festival's main purpose is to remember the departed. It is also a way to acknowledge that every living thing will face death eventually. You can enjoy a silent dinner during this time while honoring the dead by creating an altar specifically designed for them.

You may want to dedicate a special altar for them and fill it up with pictures of your departed loved ones. Add their personal items, some candles, and their favorite foods, too.

You can also offer pomegranates and apples. According to the Wiccans, pomegranates represent life, while apples represent death. Offering any of these fruits will represent the balance and harmony between the two, which is what Samhain celebrates.

Once you have already set up the altar, do the following:
- Light up a candle in memory of your departed loved one. While doing so, speak the name/s aloud. Express your gratitude and well wishes. Thank them for becoming a part of your lineage and

life.
- Sit calmly and quietly. Pay close attention to the experience and your feelings.
- Take note of any message that you think you received while doing this ritual in your journal.

Guiding the spirits is also another way to celebrate Samhain. Put a white 7-day candle in your window. This should help guide the departed to the spiritual world. Light the candle, then say the following,

"Oh little flame burning so brightly
Serve as a beacon during this night
Let your light shine the path for the dead
So they will see what is ahead
Lead and guide them to Summerland
Continue shining until Pan holds their hands
Please let your light give them peace
So they can sleep and rest with ease

This ritual should guide your departed loved ones to the right path, allowing them to get into the spiritual world in peace.

Chapter 9 – Health, Wealth, and Abundance Spells

Health and wealth are probably among the results you are aiming for when casting spells. As a witchcraft practitioner, you are probably aware that you need to stay healthy to continue learning and growing wisely. If your body is unhealthy, your spiritual body and mental health will be affected, too. This may trigger problems at various levels.

Wealth and abundance are also among the common goals of spellcasters. You may also want to cast spells for wealth, especially if you are currently unhappy with your financial situation. There is nothing more frustrating than spending a lot of time and effort in your job and then noticing your whole paycheck being consumed by your bills and debts.

It is time to make some improvements in these major areas of your life. In this chapter, you will learn some of the most effective spells you can cast so you can improve your health and attract wealth and abundance.

Preparing for the Spells

Before learning some of the most practical and effective health, wealth, and abundance spells, it is important to prepare yourself for the practice first. Note that you can't expect the spells to give you the results you want if you are not fully prepared to do it. This is even more important when casting spells for wealth and abundance.

One way to prepare for the casting of the spells is to release any negativity surrounding money and health. You have to banish all negative energies that surround you and your connection with wealth and abundance.

Keep in mind that it would be much easier for wealth and abundance to come to you if you were calm, healthy, and centered, instead of being toxic, unhealthy, stressed, and imbalanced. This means that wealth and abundance also come hand in hand with health. You also have to let go of all the negativity to increase your chances of casting the spells more effectively.

If you feel like there is negative energy surrounding you as far as money and wealth are concerned, identify its source. You should then work on healing your heart so you can look at money and wealth in a much more positive light. Cast a protection spell around you so you can get rid of all negative influences. The good news is that these protection spells are not that hard to do.

Once you have done that, expect to feel happier and calmer, which is the key to attracting better health, wealth, and abundance. Once you have released yourself from all the negativity, it is safe to say that you are prepared for the spells. The next thing you should do, therefore, is to set up the scene that will support your spellcasting.

How to Set Up the Altar for your Health and Wealth Spells?

Before casting health and wealth spells, it is crucial for you to have the appropriate surroundings. In most cases, the spells are cast at an altar, which will serve as your workspace for all your spellwork.

Fortunately, it is not that difficult to create an altar. It is even possible for you to construct yours with just a small table. Just make sure that you will not be using this table for other purposes. It also helps to make the altar portable. That way, you can easily bring it outside every time you cast spells or put it away when unused.

The altar also needs to be personal. It should be reflective of your beliefs. Here are the things that you can do to set it up more effectively.

- Get a cloth that you like, then use it to cover the surface – Once covered, you can start putting and arranging items on the altar that reflect or ignite your faith.

- Put some symbols of the four elements in your altar – Line them up based on the four principal directions. For instance, in the north, put a bowl containing sand or soil to represent the earth. You may also want to put an incense stick for air in the east, a piece of charcoal or candle for fire in the south, and a bowl containing water in the west.

- Use goddess candles – Aside from goddess candles, you may also put some ideals recognized for playing a vital role in your tradition. Set up and organize your altar using the items already mentioned. You may also want to put some tools that you plan to use in your health and wealth spells on the altar.

The main goal for setting up your altar is to develop an atmosphere designed to mentally prepare you for the spell. Also, note that every item you put on the altar can help in focusing and directing your thoughts. The higher level of focus you hold as you cast your spell, the stronger it will become, further maximizing its benefits.

Practical Health Spells

Now, it's time to learn some of the spells you can cast to improve your health. The good thing about these health spells is that they can help in healing your stress and pain, as well as that of your loved ones.

Before you start with the spells, though, make sure that you completely understand how to cast them. Make sure that you are also in a good mood since it will be you who will organize the ritual and cast the spell. You need to be in the healthiest state of mind so you can attract and deliver only positive energies.

Health and Healing Spell with Bay Leaves

If you are interested in using herbs for your health spells, then among your best choices are bay leaves. The leaves hold magical power that you can use for a wide range of purposes, including healing, cleansing, and protection. The best time to perform this spell is during the new moon.

What You Need

- 3 bay leaves
- Pen or pencil
- A piece of paper

Instructions
1. Write down your intention or wish on the paper during the new moon. For instance, since you would like to improve your health and heal, you should write your name and then cross it using your petition for healing.
2. Visualize your intention or wish coming into reality.
3. Fold the piece of paper into thirds. Put the bay leaves inside. Fold it towards you, then visualize your wish coming true.
4. Form an envelope by folding the paper into thirds again.
5. Put the folded paper in a dark place that's hidden from others. If you notice your wish coming true, burn it. This should serve as your way of showing gratitude.

Health Spell During a Waning Moon

This is a health spell that you can cast for someone else. You should do it at night during a waning moon to maximize its effects.

What You Need
- 6 bay leaves
- 6 white candles
- Incense burner
- 1 patchouli incense stick

Instructions
1. Form a circle using the white candles on the ground.
2. Light the incense stick in the middle of the formed circles. Surround it with bay leaves, too.
3. Meditate. Do this until you enjoy a sense of peace and calmness. Whisper this chant but make sure that your voice is clear.

    "May the health of (state the name of the person) increase and improve

    By the 3 by 3 power, heal him

    Rescue him from that awful disease."
4. Meditate and visualize the realization of your goal – Do this until the lighted incense burns completely.

When casting this spell, it also helps to focus your thoughts on the person who requires healing. Think about his/her good deeds and qualities, too, as you focus on the peace and silence brought on by the moment.

Spell to Maintain Good Health

If you are already in good health and you want to stay that way forever, then you can perform this spell. It is not too hard to do, and the things you need are simple. You can also use this spell anytime you feel discouraged or weak.

What You Need

- 3 candles – Use white, bright red, and light blue candles.
- 1 knife

Instructions

1. Use the knife to carve your name on each candle.
2. Once done, form a triangle on the floor using the candles with your carved name. Light the candles one by one.
3. As you light the white candle, say this loudly and clearly,

    "With the light and power of this candle, I will be protected from illness."

4. For the red candle, chant this,

    "This candle will lift and raise my strength."

5. When lighting the blue candle, say this loudly,

    "With this candle, I will remain in good health."

6. Meditate. Once you have lighted all the candles and said all the statements, you should spend time meditating. Snuff off each candle after several minutes.
7. Set the candles aside so you can cast the same spell again the next week or month.

Spell for Depression

Depression is one of the most common psychological and mental health issues affecting a lot of people at present. If you feel like you are depressed and your case is not that severe, you can perform this spell to calm you down and reduce your level of depression.

What You Need

- 1 pine cone (if you are a man) or angelica root (if you are a woman)

- Rosemary incense branch
- Sage essential oil
- Red flannel bag
- White candle
- Paper and pen

Instructions

1. Make an amulet – For you to perform this spell, you need to make an amulet, one that can help fight depression. For women, they need to carve their initials on the angelica root. Use sage oil to dress it afterward. For men, adding several drops of sage essential oil to the cone would suffice.
2. Draw a small dog using paper and pen – While drawing the figure, say the following,

    "By the power and help of this canine, I will be filled with good health."
3. Put the items you have already used in the flannel bag – After that, light the candle and incense.
4. Close the bag, then let it pass over the candle thrice – Imagine yourself feeling completely happy, smiling, and healthy. You can also do it for another person. Just imagine him/her with that positive aura, too.
5. If you are doing it for another person, deliver the red bag to him/her once the spell ends – Encourage him/her to bring this bag all the time.

After just a week, expect a major improvement in your mood and health or that of the other person.

Money, Wealth, and Abundance Spells

If your goal is to draw in energy that will give you more wealth and abundance, there are also certain spells and rituals for that. A few of the wealth and abundance spells that can give you incredible results are below.

Money Spell

This basic candle spell is one that you can do anytime. Still, it would be best to do it at a similar time every day.

What You Need
- 1 unburnt green candle, which represents wealth and money you intend to attract/acquire
- 1 unburnt white candle, which symbolizes you
- Your preferred oil

Instructions
1. Charge or anoint the candles by smearing or rubbing your chosen oil into them. While doing this step, focus on your goal or intention. Visualize the money and wealth you are about to receive.
2. Put the anointed candles on your altar. Arrange them in such a way that they are nine inches apart. The exact position of the candles is not that necessary. What is important here is that the two should be apart by 9 inches.
3. Light the candles while chanting the following words,

   "Money and wealth, come to me

   Come to me abundantly, three times three

   Enrich me financially in the best way possible

   Without harming anyone and anything along the way

   This financial abundance, I gladly accept, so mote it be
4. While chanting, move the white candle closer to green. Move it just one inch closer.
5. Blow out the flames once you are done with chanting.
6. Repeat this money spell for 9 days – moving the candle an inch closer every day. Make sure that you constantly visualize the money and wealth you intend to receive as you take every step.
7. The spell will finally be complete once you reach the 9th day, the time when the two candles touch. During the last day of the spell, allow the candles to burn until nothing is already left.

Green Candle Money Spell

This money spell that uses a green candle is also a favorite of many. You can cast it to help you finally enjoy financial abundance.

What You Need
- 1 green candle

- 6 coins – The coins can be silver, copper, or gold.
- Cinnamon
- Green pouch or cloth
- Your preferred oil

Instructions
1. Prepare the altar where you often conduct your spells. If you want, you can meditate for a while before you finally cast the spell. Meditating for even just a couple of minutes can help energize you mentally, making you fully prepared for the spell ahead.
2. Use the oil to charge or anoint the candle. After that, put it on the altar.
3. Put the coins on the altar, too. Form a circle from the coins, making them surround the candle.
4. While placing the coins, visualize already receiving the money. Project the act of gratefulness, too.
5. Light the anointed candle, then chant the following thrice,

   "Money flows, money grows;

   My money shines;

   I own this money now."
6. Lay out the pouch or cloth, then sprinkle cinnamon on it.
7. Wrap or put the coins into the pouch or cloth. While picking up the coins, chant the following words thrice,

   "Bring money to me three times three,

   Money comes from my will;

   So mote it be."
8. In case you use a cloth, bring both ends together. Form a bag out of it by tying the ends. Carry it with you all the time, then visualize yourself as you receive your desired money.

Financial Aid Spell

This spell should help you during those times when you are desperately in need of financial aid.

What You Need
- 2 green candles
- 1 gold candle

- Fire-proof container
- Soft incense

Instructions

1. Light both candles. With the candles lighted up, meditate on the beauty and wonders of living without worrying about bills. Begin with the bill you intend to settle in full the most. From there, you can move down the bills on your list.
2. Create a statement that resembles a bill on a piece of paper. Write down the total bill amount and anything else that will make this piece of paper look like a real bill.
3. Focus on it for one minute or so as you imagine that specific amount of money.
4. Get a red marker or pen and use it to write "PAID IN FULL" across the bill. All letters should be capitalized.
5. Burn the bill while visualizing your will to pay the amount in full coming into reality.

Full Moon Money Spell

The full moon is so powerful that it can boost a lot of spells. Note, though, that there are specific rituals that you have to perform during a full moon to make them even more effective. Harness the lunar power even more through this money spell.

What You Need

- Water
- Cauldron
- Silver coin

Instructions

1. During the full moon, specifically at night, get your cauldron, then fill it with water. It should be half-full.
2. Put the silver coin inside the cauldron.
3. After that, position the cauldron in such a way that the light of the moon shines over the water. Chant the following thrice,

    "Enchanting and powerful Lady of the Moon

    Let your wealth flow to me quite soon

    Gold and silver, I will them to fill my hands

> *Everything you can bring to me*
> *My purse can hold."*

4. After chanting, you can pour the water into the ground. Put the silver coin in your purse or pocket so you can keep it close to you all the time.

Chapter 10 – Love Spells and Charms

Probably the most popular reason for wanting to know how to cast spells is to attract love and romance; that's what this final chapter of the book will cover. Of course, almost everyone wants to experience love. It is the most positive feeling that you can experience and share.

However, it is not also a secret that there are several times when love and relationships become tricky and challenging. This is especially true if the one you dream of does not seem to notice you. If you are particularly experiencing challenges as far as love, relationships, and romance are concerned, then you may seek the help of love spells and charms.

Attraction Spell

This love spell is meant to attract the person you love and desire. You don't have to worry when casting this spell, as you can easily do it at home. In addition, it does not aim to manipulate the mind of another person or trigger changes to all the things that revolve around you. What it does is help you leave a good impression on the one you like so he/she will notice you.

What You Need
- 2 candles
- A piece of white paper
- A pen

Instructions
1. Sit in a quiet and peaceful room. Make sure that you are calm and comfortable enough as you sit there. Focus on your intention while in that position.
2. Get rid of all the distractions on your mind. The goal here is to attain mental clarity so you can make this spell work in your favor.
3. Once your mind is free from all distractions and other unnecessary thoughts, get the paper and pen, so you can start writing down your intention.
4. Light the two candles. Allow the paper to catch the flame from the candles.
5. Look at the flame while chanting the following words as many times as possible,

    "*May a special someone see and notice me today*

    May I be blessed today without harming anyone on the way"
6. Take the ashes out so the wind can swallow them up. Never blow out the candles after doing the steps. Let them die down naturally.

It is advisable to perform this attraction spell continuously nine times. This is so you can attain your desired outcome.

Love Spell to Make an Ex Come Back

If you have an ex whom you still love, you can use this love spell. Just like the other spell we have already provided, this one is safe, meaning it will never cause harm to another person. It will not also attract bad karma.

Note, though, that instead of forcing your ex to love you again, this powerful love spell aims to remove the negative and toxic energy that may cause the gap between you and your ex. In addition, this magic can make you more attractive and appealing than before, thereby helping you draw your ex back to you.

What You Need
- 2 white pillar candles
- Sage smudge
- 1 purple candle

Instructions

1. Meditate for a few minutes first. This should help in clearing your mind from every chaos and stress that you have been experiencing every day.
2. Light one of the white candles while saying,
   "This candle is my divine self."
3. Hold the candle with both your hands.
4. Light the other candle while saying,
   "This is the divine self of (state the name of your ex-lover)."
5. Light the remaining candle, which is the purple one, while saying,
   "May we receive guidance to reach our highest good."
6. Imagine the scene wherein the two of you enjoy a harmonious and happy moment together. It should not have any requirement for attachment, though.
7. Prepare the sage smudge and burn it. Blow the burned sage over all the candles.
8. Think of the conflicts that the two of you had before, then say the following aloud while there is still smoke,
   "And there is no harm
   So mote it be."
9. Blow out all the lighted candles.

Do the spell and ritual again for seven consecutive days. Avoid showing that you desperately want your ex to go back to you, though.

Spell to Attract New Love

For this love spell and charm, you will need to use lepidolite, a lilac crystal capable of filling your heart with the expansive and nice feeling of being in love. Letting yourself become in tune with this specific frequency and feeling can help you become a magnet for such a condition.

What You Need

- Lepidolite crystal
- Full or waxing moon

Instructions

1. Cleanse the lepidolite crystal. You can do the cleansing by holding the crystal either in the light produced by the full or waxing moon or the bright sunlight.
2. Allow the crystal to bathe in the light for one to two minutes.
3. With your right hand, hold the crystal close to your heart.
4. Breathe and relax. Allow the feeling of joy brought on by meeting someone new who delights your heart and reciprocates that feeling.
5. Be grateful for the feeling and the condition of being in love. It should be as if the condition is already one hundred percent true.
6. Keep the love charm close to your heart every time you go out. Anytime soon, you will be able to meet someone new who will be your potential partner.

Love Spell to Find Your Match

Are you desperately in search of your ideal match? Do you want to finally find your "the one"? Then this love spell could be the ultimate solution.

What You Need

- New vanilla extract bottle
- Paper
- 2 rose thorns
- 3 white candles

Instructions

1. Buy a new vanilla extract bottle. Open it by removing the lid.
2. Write your name on the paper, then put the rose thorns on it.
3. Light the white candles. After that, place the lighted candles around the bottle.
4. Let your sight focus on the light of the candles. While doing that, think of your desire to find your true mate. Also, chant the following,

    "Red like blood,

    Enliven my romantic relationship,

    Bring love and romance to me soon,

Give me love as lasting as my surname,
As I will it, I will find the right person."

5. Sprinkle a few drops of vanilla extract in your room. This should help in sealing the love spells. Make sure to cap the bottle of vanilla tightly, then put it under your bed.

Love Spell to Make your Marriage Last

This love spell is meant for those who are already married but want to make their relationship as long-lasting as possible. This should also help you retain the fire and passion in your relationship.

With that, it can contribute to having a successful married life. It would be best to cast this spell when the full moon is around. Put it somewhere, either outside or inside, where you get the chance to see the moon. In case of overcast, choose another night.

What You Need

- A silver ring – It does not have to be real silver
- A small white dish
- A fresh white rose
- Some pinches of damiana, lemon verbena, and dried yarrow

Instructions

1. One day before casting this love spell, put the silver ring in a bowl containing the dried herbs. Leave it there for one day. Do the remaining parts of the spell and ritual once the full moon comes.
2. In a standing position, face the moon. Hold the silver ring up, making it possible for you to witness the moon's glowing face through the central part of the ring.
3. Say the following words aloud,

    "Bring to me the bond I genuinely and greatly desire
    My love for my spouse will never get tired
    By the full moon's light
    Bring a successful marriage to me soon."

4. Hold the rose up. That way, you can cover the face of the moon and then repeat the steps. Drop down the ring of the rose's stem. That way, there is a high chance for the ring to sit at the flower's base.

5. Set aside the flower with the ring and put them in a bowl of herbs. Say the chant one last time.
6. Make sure to leave everything securely in place until the full moon next year. Expect to witness some good results from the spell after that.

Honey Jar Love Spell

This spell requires plenty of ingredients, but it is all worth it, considering its effectiveness.

What You Need
- Honey jar
- Parchment paper
- Paints or pens to decorate the jar
- 1 pink candle
- Some plants and herbs, like red pepper, jasmine, vanilla bean, nutmeg, bay leaves, basil, cardamom, lavender, and cinnamon.

Instructions
1. Use some salt water to cleanse the honey jar. Let it dry completely.
2. Decorate the jar while using colors that represent love, like pink and red. Draw and write any word and symbol that you can easily associate with love.
3. Write this love chant on paper, too,

    With this powerful spell, I attract someone

    The person who is my faith and destiny

    With the help of this spell I am casting tonight

    Expect love to come – one that I know is right for me.
4. Put the paper with your name on it inside the jar. Add the dried flowers and herbs that you prepared earlier.
5. Use honey to fill up the jar.
6. Put the pink candle over the honey jar. Light it.
7. Look for a private spot where you can safely do your spell and ritual. Put it there.
8. In case you wish to recharge, just put one tea light on your container, then light it.

Some Tips When Casting Love Spells

To ensure that you cast love spells and gain the best results from them, allow yourself to be guided by the tips mentioned here.

Be a true believer in magic

Note that if you focus your energy on something that helps you create lasting love, it is also highly likely that your mind will be filled with more love. Believe in this type of magic - one based specifically on spirit and faith. Maintain your faith so you can finally witness your desired results.

Be specific and open-minded

One rule when it comes to casting love spells is that you should avoid using magic as a means of forcing someone to feel something that is not natural for them. Remember that love needs to be a choice all the time. You should avoid forcing it on someone.

As you recite invocations regarding open-ended loves, do not use the names. Focus on the traits and qualities that you wish your potential partner should have - among which are being loving and caring.

Understand that love magic still has limitations

One limitation can be seen in the rule stating that you should never use love spells and white magic for a negative purpose. Also, avoid using black magic in breaking a marriage or any other thing similar to that. Make sure to use the spells only for positive purposes.

Know the perfect time to cast the love spells

If you are serious about casting love spells, learn about the perfect time to do them. Love spells tend to work better if you cast them on Fridays. The reason is that Venus day falls on a Friday. It also helps to cast spells during the new moon as this phase helps in making some new opportunities real.

Conclusion

Spellcrafting and casting are definitely one of the most satisfying things that a magic and witchcraft practitioner can do. Note that even if you are still a beginner, you can still find several ways to learn and understand how you can execute this art of crafting magic. The only thing that you need would be the right reading material and guide – one that will teach you the many steps that you have to take to be great in the world of magic and witchcraft.

Note that all spells require a few different components for them to work effectively. It is also important for you to learn about all the elements and factors that can greatly affect the results of the spells you make and cast.

Hopefully, this book has enlightened you about every important detail related to spellcrafting and spellcasting. Use everything that you have learned from this book, so you can finally consider yourself an expert practitioner in the field of witchcraft and magic.

Part 2: White Magic

The Ultimate Guide to Protection Spells, Blessings, Candle Magick, Wiccan Rituals, and Spellcrafting for Good Purposes

Introduction

Due to its ties to the Pagan culture and belief systems, white magic is one of the most natural ways to manifest a Wiccan practice. The benefits of this practice come from the way it's used for selfless purposes. Acts of white or natural magic may include everything from the simple act of bringing positivity to others' lives to healing their minds and bodies. White magic may use different symbols from different religions depending on its practitioner's background. Although Wicca is most prevalent in this practice, this craft also often incorporates elements of other belief systems. However, ultimately it all comes down to intent. In most cultures, white magic is viewed as a generous practice designed to counteract ill-intended black magic spells. From the early adaptations in the Paleolithic religion to modern-day practices, white magic has always been a powerful tool for spiritual empowerment and inner growth.

By focusing on the needs of others, you can learn compassion, love, and enough positivity to heal and transform lives – including your own. Transforming a stressful, mundane existence is only possible through nature, which is why this craft is so effective. By blessing and healing others, you are filling yourself with positive energy. As this energy accumulates inside your body and mind, you will regain all the benefits you sent out toward others and, in the process, probably gain some skills you weren't even expecting to acquire. Considering all this, it's something worth investing time and effort into – which you will definitely need to do. Like most spiritual journeys, conquering the craft of white magic in Wicca does require focus and practice.

To comprehend what it takes for a practitioner to embark on this natural Wiccan journey, you must familiarize yourself with its background. And to make the most of the craft, you will also need to understand the roles nature and one's own mind play in this process. This book will help you to do all that and much more. It contains a wealth of rituals and spells that harness the natural power of love and healing – as long as they are used for good purposes. From how to use certain objects to combat dark magic to the different ways to spread your light – here you will find everything you need for your craft. What's even better, all this comes in an incredibly beginner-friendly package.

Whatever worries you may have about your ability to embark on this path of righteousness can be allayed. Ultimately, all it takes is simply educating yourself about what it takes to become a better version of yourself. If you are a complete newcomer to Wicca, learning about this craft is a wonderful way to begin your journey. And suppose you are a well-versed practitioner who is simply looking for different spiritual fulfillment; all the more reason to turn to white magic for a solution because besides sending benefits to others, you will also learn how to celebrate yourself and your own natural strength. If you are ready to arm yourself with protection and guidance toward self-fulfillment – and do so through the selfless acts of making the world a better place – please keep reading.

Chapter 1: A Brief History of White Magic

Regardless of whether they are or aren't interested in witchcraft, most people are likely familiar with the terms white and black magic.

Black magic is the use of magic for selfish, malicious, and often evil purposes and is often also referred to as the Left-Hand Path. White magic is its counterpart, and it is used to refer to the use of magic for selfless, benevolent purposes.

Practitioners of white magic are often known as white witches, shamans, and healers, depending on the culture and the community. Most traditions of white magic focus on non-offensive magic – that is, protective magic practiced through healing rituals, blessings, protection charms and spells, and prayers, songs, and incantations.

Where black magic represents the Left-Hand Path, white magic is the Right-Hand Path. If this is your first time encountering these two types of magic, you should first understand white magic better before learning how to practice it.

The History of White Magic

Like all forms of magic, white magic can trace its origins to early religions, even as far back as the Paleolithic time period. Scholars have traced white magic traditions to the worship of fertility and vegetation deities that could be found as far back as Ancient Egypt and in the early traditions of Judaism and Christianity.

Following the advent of Christianity, witchcraft of all kinds - regardless of whether it was white or black magic - became the source of much fear and derision in Europe and Colonial America. People believed to be witches were targeted in witch trials and were often burnt at the stake or executed in some other gruesome manner.

Witch trials targeted mainly women and were not limited to genuine magic practitioners. Accusations made due to minor feuds with neighbors could often lead to execution regardless of guilt.

In the UK, the last person executed for witchcraft was in 1727. In colonial North America, witchcraft trials were primarily held in the 1600s, and accusations and prosecutions continued as late as 1883.

At the same time, however, magic was a topic of much fascination and was discussed in numerous cultural circles, especially in Europe. Certain scholars like Marsilio Ficino and his followers advocated for the existence of spirits and other spiritual beings. However, these beliefs were seen as suspect by the Roman Catholic Church.

At the same time, it couldn't be discounted that the Church also acknowledged the existence of spirits - it was this acknowledgment that formed the basis of their support for the witch trials and other campaigns against witchcraft.

The Renaissance and the 15th and 16th centuries saw a resurgence in the belief in ceremonial magic.

In the mid-1400s, Johannes Hartlieb put forth his list of the Artes *magicae* - the seven arts prohibited by canon (Church) law. This list included necromancy, which is often considered part of black (or demonic) magic. The full list included:

- **Nigromancy**: Literally meaning black magic, most modern scholars believe this referred specifically to the art of necromancy
- **Geomancy**: A form of divination that involves throwing rocks, sand, or dirt onto the ground and interpreting the resulting shapes formed. It was among the most popular forms of magic practiced during the Renaissance.
- **Hydromancy**: Divination that involves the use of water. Hydromancy is also referred to as *scrying*, performed with water as a medium.
- **Aeromancy**: A counterpart of geomancy, aeromancy involved interpreting atmospheric conditions like thunder, falling stars, and comets. Other aeromancy practices included interpreting the shapes of clouds, tossing sand or seeds into the air, and interpreting the pattern of the resultant dust cloud and/or how the seeds settled on the ground.
- **Pyromancy**: Divination by reading and interpreting the patterns and signs found in fire and flames.
- **Chiromancy**: Also known as palm reading or palmistry, this involves divination by reading the palms of people's hands.
- **Scapulimancy**: Divination using an animal's scapula. The scapula would be broken, and the patterns caused by the break would allow the practitioner to read the future.

Well-known figures of the time who were interested in magic included Leonardo da Vinci and Sir Isaac Newton. A contemporary of Hartlieb, Heinrich Cornelius Agrippa, published one of the best-known works on magic and the occult during the Renaissance, the *De occulta philosophia libri tres*.

This work contained an outline of numerous topics that would become key parts of later magic practices, including (but not limited to):

- Numerology
- Astrology
- The classical elements
- Kabbalah

The work also explored how these magical practices could be used, not only in magical rituals and ceremonies like scrying and the practice of alchemy, but it also detailed their potential use in medicine.

The impact of the fascination of the upper and scholarly classes can be seen in one of Shakespeare's most famous plays, *The Tempest*. In it, one of the main characters, Prospero, is a magician, and, it can be argued, he was a practitioner of white magic, as opposed to Sycorax and the monster Caliban, who could both be seen as representations of black magic practitioners.

Prospero is also seen as a representation of the Renaissance Magus. During the Renaissance, the Magus (or mage) was a figure who worked to understand the cosmos and humanity's position within it. Though not directly a magician, a Magus would practice several arts associated with magic, including astrology and Kabbalah.

Prospero's reference to the stars in the play indicates his interest in astrology; his control over the spirit, Ariel, also represents his control over his own magic. Though readings over his intentions as a magician and a Magus differ, it is hard for scholars to argue that Shakespeare was not influenced by contemporary beliefs in magic.

Other Shakespearean plays influenced by magic include:

- **Macbeth:** The three witches are clearly practitioners of black magic.
- **A Midsummer Night's Dream:** References fairies and other supernatural creatures performing what can be seen as magic.
- **Hamlet:** Though there is no direct reference to magic, the ghost of Hamlet's father adds a tinge of magical influence to the play.

At the same time, it should be noted that belief in, and celebration of, magic remained a perilous undertaking, especially in Britain. Under Elizabeth I, the magician John Dee was given prominence.

However, Dee's magic was known as "natural magic" or magic without the influence of spirits. Natural magic was seen as a partner to the Christian God rather than being in opposition with him. For example, natural magicians would use their knowledge and powers to heal with medicine or calculate the right time for a harvest through their understanding of astrology. Dee helped determine the most auspicious date for the coronation of Elizabeth I.

Even natural magic came under threat in Britain following the coronation of James VI. He believed that female communities threatened his political power and used the fear of witchcraft to call for prosecutions of "witches," including using execution as a suitable punishment. Dee himself was forced to argue that his practices did not oppose the will of God, and he died in poverty before The Tempest was written.

Given this concern and the approaching witch trials, most authors explicitly distanced themselves from the practice of (and interest in) witchcraft and magic, especially in the seven Artes magicae detailed above. Even Agrippa rejected all forms of ceremonial magic.

The interest in magic and the occult during the Renaissance had a twofold effect:

On the one hand, some scholars argue that this interest allowed the witch trials to continue as late as the 18th century. It was only after belief in magic and witchcraft stopped being part of the mainstream that the trails truly started to draw to a close.

At the same time, Gareth Knight, author of *A History of White Magic*, and Paola Zambelli, author of *White Magic, Black Magic in the European Renaissance*, argue that the philosophical thinking on magic during the Renaissance helped develop the modern traditions of white magic. This includes the symbolism of the star, which would develop into the contemporary pentagram. Additionally, Zambelli also argued that the study of the occult and magic during this period helped make white magic palatable to the greater population. The theories of natural magic helped set it strictly in contrast to black (and, therefore, evil and demonic) magic.

White Witches and the Cunning Folk

Alongside the scholarly thinking on the occult existed the tradition of cunning folk, folk healers, and white witches across Europe and America.

In these communities (usually rural or outside of major cities), the terms "witch" and "witchcraft" were intrinsically associated with harmful black magic rather than being divided into white and black magic.

However, they also believed in positive magic, and practitioners of this helpful magic were referred to varyingly as:

- Cunning folk
- Wise people (wise men or wise women)
- Medicine men
- Witch doctors (most commonly in Africa)
- "Unbinding," "good," or "white" witches
- Pellars and dyn hysbys (in Britain)

Folk magicians are found across the world, and names for them in other languages include:

- Curanderos in Latin America and some parts of Spain
- Benandanti in Italy
- Devins-guérisseurs and leveurs de sorts in France
- Bean Feasa, banfháidh, and fáidhbhean in Ireland
- Vedmak among the Slavic peoples
- Kloge folk in Denmark
- Hexenmeister in Germany

These practitioners were often highly respected, and they offered numerous services to their communities, including:

- **Healing:** In rural communities particularly, folk healers were often the only medical practitioners available to help with injuries and illnesses. Also, folk healers and white magic practitioners were consulted for medical help with livestock and other animals.
- **Love magic**
- **Divination**
- **Finding lost and/or stolen property**

- **Breaking or Countering the Effects of Harmful Magic:** Perhaps the most common service offered by folk magicians, these folk magicians were also occasionally approached to help people identify malicious witches. Combating the effects of witchcraft usually required a combination of herbal medicine, written charms, prayers, magic rituals, and more. Some common charms and rituals used to identify and counter malicious witchcraft include using witch bottles (ceramic bottles filled with certain body parts of the victim, like hair and nail clippings), sticking nails into an effigy of the suspected witch, and more.

The magic that these folk magicians and white witches performed is often referred to as low magic and stands in contrast to high (or ceremonial) magic. That said, some folk magicians would often incorporate certain elements of high magic into their practices, especially those involved with the esoteric study.

As mentioned above, cunning folk and folk magicians were commonly found in rural communities, and most – if not all – of them were Christians by religion and did not see themselves as witches or magicians. However, they were among the most commonly accused of witchcraft during the witch trials, especially in early witch trials across Europe. For example, some estimates claim that over half of the people accused of witchcraft in Hungary were actually healers or practitioners of other folk magic.

Aside from the services mentioned above, folk magicians had their own magical practices. These included:

- **Spellcasting and Charms:** These often took the form of written charms and were used to find love or protect the bearer from harmful witchcraft. The words that constituted the charms were believed to have magical powers, usually found in grimoires (usually magic words, such as the famous Abracadabra or the term sator arepo tenet opera rotas) or in the Bible (such as one of the names of God or the angels, or quoted sections of the Bible in non-English languages such as Greek or Latin). These charms were either worn on the bearer's person or placed in their home. Other common charms included ones that involved the bones of toads (or frogs).

- **Grimoires:** Grimoires were printed books of magic or on the occult. Though grimoires had been around since medieval times, they cost a lot to produce, as they had to be written out by hand. The invention of the printing press made them far more accessible to common people. Significant grimoires included Cornelius Agrippa's Three Books of Occult Philosophy and Reginald Scot's Discoverie of Witchcraft.

- **Familiar Spirits:** Some folk magicians were said to employ the help of familiar spirits in their practice of magic. These spirits were also thought to work for more sinister witches and were often associated with nature. Spirits were said to remember the personalities of their masters – those belonging to folk healers and magicians were benevolent. In contrast, those belonging to witches were malevolent and dangerous. They were distinguished by being called either "fairies" (good) or "demons" (bad). Familiar spirits were commonly described as appearing out of nowhere, inherited from other magical practitioners, or given a more powerful spirit to the practitioner. They were believed to take the practitioner on a journey to Elfhame or Fairyland, where they would feast and celebrate with the rest of the fairies. Some scholars believe this description of a journey is connected to the celebration of the sabbats. All familiar spirits were branded as demons or demonic during the witch trials.

- **Christianity:** As mentioned above, a wide majority of the folk healers and magicians in Europe and America were Christians themselves. Religion played a major influence in their magical practices. For example, it was common to use Bible quotes and religious words in written charms. Surviving spells from the period also show clear Christian influences, going as far as invoking God in the spell.

This tradition of folk healers and folk magicians also led to the creation of hereditary lines, in which the power and knowledge of white magic are passed down either through a biological connection or direct tutelage from a well-known white magician or folk healer.

Modern White Magic Beliefs

Modern white magic is commonly associated with the worship of the mother goddess and a reverence for nature. Indeed, white magic is closely associated with Wicca. Like Wicca, white magic sees Nature as divine in itself.

The use of white magic is an experience in personal growth. Most white magic practitioners eschew any harmful actions, as they believe in putting out only positive energy in the world.

It is the precise opposite of black magic. White magic focuses on:
- Healing
- Helping people
- Blessings
- Protective charms, spells, and incantations
- Prayers and songs meant to benefit others

Black magic, on the other hand, involves:
- Working with evil spirits
- xNecromancy
- Curses and hexes intended to harm the victim.
- True name spells, based on the theory that knowing a person's true name gives a practitioner complete control over the person
- Immortality rituals, which go against the natural order of life and death

Additionally, black magic practitioners may also work with demons or be involved with Satanism and other forms of devil worship.

Indeed, many white magic practitioners believe in both the Wiccan Rede and the Rule of Three.

The Wiccan Rede

The Wiccan Rede essentially serves as the main moral system in Wicca and other witchcraft traditions that use similar practices, including white magic as a whole. There are two forms of the Rede - a longer rede, which essentially takes the form of a poem, and the more common eight words rede, which reads:

"An ye harm none, do what ye will."

This essentially translates to "As long as you harm no one, do what you want to."

However, it should be noted that not all Wiccans follow the Rede, and many believe it is merely advice rather than a true "rule" or commandment that is to be followed. They believe that the Rede is a guideline that essentially tells people to "do no harm" – and it is up to the individual in question to determine what doing harm means. Thus, what one person may see harm may not be seen as malevolent or harmful to another person.

Other interpretations read the Rede as an encouragement for people to follow their True Will, rather than trying to use magic to obtain simple wants. It is a reminder that practitioners should take responsibility for their actions and how their use of magic impacts themselves and the people around them.

Additionally, traditional interpretations of the Rede don't just include doing no harm to other people and creatures – it also covers doing no harm to oneself.

Law of Threefold Return

Also known as the Rule of Three, the Threefold Law, or the Law of Return, the Law of Threefold Return essentially states that all energy that a practitioner puts out into the world will return to them three times over. This applies to both positive and negative energies and is not merely limited to magic but to all energy as a whole.

Along with the Wiccan Rede, the Law of Threefold Return is a crucial part of the moral system followed by Wiccans, white magic practitioners, Neo-Pagans, and several other occult traditions. That said, like the Rede, it is not universally observed by all Wiccans, and some practitioners simply see the Law of Threefold Return as an expanded form of the Rede.

Many practitioners and scholars see the Law of Threefold Return as a punishment and reward system similar to that found in several other religions. Some traditions also believe that the Rule of Three is not as literal as described above. Rather, they believe that it is a symbolic statement that the energy a person puts out into the world will return to them **as many times as are necessary** until they learn the lesson that the universe is trying to teach them.

White magic can seem intimidating for new practitioners, especially as not all practitioners of white magic are Wiccans. However, it is possible to get into it with a little study and application and – most importantly – the desire to help other people.

The rest of this book will help you learn how to start practicing white magic. It will cover the basics of white magic and help you understand how to apply white magic and spells in a practical way in your everyday life. It will provide you with hands-on techniques and methods to banish negative energies.

If you're looking to get started with white magic, read on to the next chapter, which covers following Wicca as a part of white magic.

Chapter 2: Getting Started with Wicca: A White Magic Craft

This chapter is dedicated to helping you start your magical journey practicing Wicca as a form of white magic. After all, Wicca is one of the most elemental forms of practice that draws power from nature. Similar to white magic, it's primarily intended for benevolent purposes. Therefore, learning the basics of Wiccan witchcraft can be a great stepping stone toward developing your craft and making a positive change in this world. However, before you dive into the world of Wicca, you will need to familiarize yourself with a few basic terms, rituals, and tools used in this craft.

Wicca and Magick

The term magick was coined by occultist Aleister Crowley, the founder of Thelema. While the word originates from the term magic, it's deliberately spelled differently to differentiate occult religions from theater magic, which Crowley considered a mere illusion. While nowadays we could hardly confuse Wiccan or similar practices with stage acts, in the early 1900s, this was a common occurrence. Crowley found it necessary to make a clear distinction to persuade his followers to learn the differences between the two. In addition, by expanding the word magic to "magick," Crowley created a six-lettered word, which had a huge significance in occult practices. The number six is present in several occult symbols, including the hexagram often used in Thelema and Wicca.

According to Crowley, rituals of magick are nothing more than the practitioner's acts of will, and the results of the rituals are the consequence of changing in the conformity of this will. He also stressed that one doesn't have to be versed in the craft to perform a change – as long as the person wants something to happen and it's possible by nature, it will happen. Crowley defined this power as "true will," which essentially represents the expression of nonconformity to one's destiny. Therefore, magick is a great tool for self-discovery, which is one of the reasons why this concept was adopted by other practices, including Wicca. Whether you are a beginner or a seasoned practitioner, Wiccan magick can help you find your path in life.

If you want to gain assurance of your purposes, practicing Wicca – and white magic in particular – will provide you with the necessary guidance. Through it, you can discover the proper course to follow. Most importantly, you will gain the required wisdom to stay on the right path. Knowing which aspects of your life are hindering your success is only possible through nature, eliminating these obstacles from your path. The selflessness of white magic is a wonderful way to develop the parts of your spirit responsible for balance and happiness in your life.

While you may rely on the guidance from several deities, in Wiccan practices, the driving force remains your own power. Whether you choose to use Gods and Goddesses for devotion will be up to you, but they can definitely enrich your practice. However, they are only helpful if you also learn how to control the universal energy which connects you with nature. Choose to devote yourself to the craft of white magic. You may use this natural energy to achieve things in your day-to-day life, alongside other magick practices.

White Magic in Wicca

Like Wicca, white magic is also a practice that relies on natural forces and provides spiritual strength to the practitioner. Nature is represented in the Craft through polarized divine forces, which can be a God and a Goddess, a day and night, sun and moon, and many more. Whichever forces you choose to use in your practice, make sure you respect all its elements - as well as the opposing forces. It's also a good idea to stay connected to nature at all times so that you can draw strength from it. Living in the city may make this quite a challenge, but there is always a solution if you look hard enough. From taking frequent camping trips to the country or surrounding yourself with indoor plants, there are many ways to incorporate nature into your life.

One of the major benefits of Wicca is that despite all the generosity it offers, it's a practice that comes with very few rules. As long as it doesn't do any harm to you or anyone else, pretty much everything is permitted. Many Wiccans believe that casting negative magick causes three times the harm, so you want to avoid doing that. Positive magick may very well result in triple benefits, which means more power for you. Even if you will literally benefit in the same way as the person towards whom the spell is directed, you are still doing a good deed and growing personally - which is the ultimate goal of white magic practitioners. Naturally, holding this power comes with enormous responsibility, as every one of your decisions can benefit your own fate as well as that of others.

Whichever way you are directing your craft, white magic may improve someone's life in more ways than one. Whether you cast a benevolent spell for monetary gain or to recover from an illness - as long as you achieve results through natural means, you will be able to succeed. There is always spiritual healing at the base of all this, which has no boundaries. It doesn't seem like it initially, but with white magic, you can overcome every roadblock far more easily.

How to Start Practicing White Magic

As a beginner, you may have trouble focusing your energy on manifesting your intentions. While it's not a prerequisite to a successful practice, having an altar can help you channel your magick. If you decide to set up an altar, make sure you do it in a space where you can relax and concentrate on what you want to manifest. An altar can be anything from a nightstand in your bedroom to a storage chest in your living room - as long as it provides a large enough flat surface on which to place your tools, it will work. Since white magic relies on natural forces, it's a good idea to use a wooden altar so that you can be that much closer to nature. Likewise, a good amount of natural light will be necessary for letting the energy flow more freely. If your practice involves a specific element or natural polarity, you need to set up an altar accordingly. For example, when working with the four directions, you must place the altar facing the direction you are expecting the benefits from. A craft that relies on creation may prove fruitful when practiced in the kitchen.

When it comes to getting the tools for your altar, which ones you need will mostly depend on your individual preferences. For example, if you are working with a particular deity, you need to have their symbol at the altar. Common symbols used in Wiccan practices are the Mother Goddess and the Horned God. They can be symbolized as statues or items that have been associated with them in different traditions. Whether used for working with a deity or not, candles are also great to have on your altar. A great way to incorporate nature into your craft is by representing the four elements at the altar.

For this, you will need natural items, which you can arrange based on the four cardinal directions, alongside a candle in an appropriate color:

- You can represent Earth on the North with stone, plants, salt, raw food, a pentacle, and a light green or yellow candle.
- Fire in the form of a candle, oils, or a knife should face the South, together with a red candle.
- Place a feather, a wand, a bell, or a wand and light blue candle to the East to represent Air.
- Use a glass of water or wine, a seashell, or a cauldron, with a green or blue candle on the West to symbolize Water.

While these objects symbolize the natural forces, other items you may need refer to your own power and intention. Their meaning can also be determined by your background and traditions, as it's you who should benefit the most. Healers use herbs, while others require other elements.

When working at the altar, you will need to be mindful of a couple of things. For it to be fruitful, white magic should always be positive and performed solely for the good of others. And while it often encourages emotional and physical healing, achieving inner peace, and personal growth in others, white magic will never disregard their will. Trying to cast a spell that goes against someone's wishes while benefiting you is not white magic.

Casting a circle is the second fundamental step every new witch should learn. To do this, you will need either something to draw with or small objects you can place around your altar, forming a circular shape. From crystals to twigs to people joining hands – everything can work.

Once your altar is set – and you have channeled all the energy you need, you can perform the intended spell, ritual, or other activity, like meditation. When using a spell, make sure it has a positive tone and is entirely without violence. While memorizing an incantation before reciting it may help you to focus more, in the beginning, you may rely on written aids instead.

Mediation

Meditation exercises often lead to a better understanding of the elements and forces the Wiccan witch deals with. Furthermore, they are a great way to clear your mind of the clutter of everyday life, leaving you free to focus on what you want to manifest. To manifest white magick, you must align yourself with nature, and to do this, you will need to be relaxed.

Meditation can teach you how to reach a state of relaxation in your mind and channel your thoughts in the right direction. Stilling your mind and body allows you to get in touch with your inner spirit – but this is only possible to do with lots of practice. You don't have to do long séances, but doing it on a day-to-day basis will be beneficial.

The best thing about meditation is that you can tailor it to your needs and preferences. Whether you do it in front of your altar, in a park, or while waiting in a queue, it will work anywhere. For beginners, it's recommended to do it in a quiet place, preferably close to nature. Make sure you can assume a comfortable position because if your body can't relax, neither will your mind. When choosing your approach, you will have two options. You can either opt for a passive mediation technique, where you still your mind and wait until the thought you want to manifest rises, or take an active approach and focus on a symbol until it evokes those thoughts.

A common meditation exercise you may use as a beginner is simply closing your eyes and focusing on the rise of your chest without modifying your breathing. Your body is part of nature, and becoming aware of its function will help you connect to natural energy. Make sure that after your chest, you also examine the state of other parts of your body. When doing so, don't focus on any particular idea, even if you perceive any tension. Only after you have become aware of how the energy flows through your body should you begin focusing on melting away any tension.

Once there is no more blockage within your body, start focusing on your breathing again. If a particular thought arises when switching focus, don't give it any attention yet. It may be a particularly nagging one – in which case you will have to do your best to let it go. Remember, you must stay in the present. Otherwise, you won't be able to manifest anything now. To do this, take several deep breaths until your mind releases those thoughts. Try to visualize whatever you were worrying about as if it were leaving your body with each exhale.

Having learned how to empty your mind, now you can move on to more complex meditation exercises. When you have reached a relaxed state, open your conscious mind to whatever your subconscious may present it with. Whether it's a symbol you are trying to manifest, a deity that's trying to reach you, or nature itself, you will probably receive a message in this state. Some meditation subjects recommended new witches delve into white magick to revolve their minds around change and how it causes personal growth. You may also want to focus on what your mind will achieve when you train it to manifest your intentions.

Practicing Solitary vs. in a Coven

As a beginner, one of the best ways to learn about the craft is from fellow Wiccans. Joining a coven consisting of experienced practitioners can help you start on your journey as you will always have someone with whom to share your experiences. Wiccan covens are usually quite flexible, and while some members may hold more wisdom, there is no distinguished hierarchy. They typically only informally invite people to their celebrations, and there is no obligatory attendance. If you feel that a particular ritual doesn't sit comfortably with your values, or you are just too busy to attend, you can stay away from it. Most covens consist of three to five witches, but they are open to inviting guests as well, particularly if it's a person who wants to learn more about the craft. Whether one becomes a permanent member or not, they will go through a process of initiation, which serves as spiritual cleansing. However, staying in a coven may be too restricting for some practitioners. If your main purpose is to discover and fulfill your destiny, your craft should emphasize your own goals. Albeit very helpful in initial spiritual guidance, covens typically work for common purposes, which may hinder your personal goal fulfillment.

On the other hand, learning how to get started with Wiccan practices on your own can be quite challenging, and more so if you want to use white magic. Unlike its black counterpart, the resources for white magic are often less comprehensive, and the practice itself seems to have less importance. Practicing solo means finding all the resources and tools for your rituals on your own. Furthermore, you are obligated to rely on yourself (and nature) for spiritual guidance. However, due to the nature-based concept of white magic, the solitary path may teach you more about your own powers than any teacher could. Naturally, being a solitary practitioner does not preclude you from sharing your experience with fellow witches either. In fact, most modern Wiccans begin their practices as either a temporary member of a coven or with a friend or family member who shares their interests and beliefs. By sharing common experiences, you can learn new practices and carry on to your day-to-day life, even after you are no longer part of the coven or group. You can always meet up with others when you find a spiritual connection with another witch.

Final Words of Wisdom

When beginning to practice this craft, the most important thing to keep in mind is that white magic is the manifestation of your intentions. Through it, you can focus your energy and the natural energy around you on making your desires into reality. While the ultimate goal is to find self-fulfillment, this craft is about how you are getting there. White magic teaches you that doing the things that make you happy will ultimately attract even more success. A positive approach and white magic go hand in hand because you cannot expect beneficial outcomes and fulfillment if your mind is filled with negative thoughts. Apart from adopting a kinder attitude toward yourself, this also means learning how to be more compassionate toward others. Furthermore, being calm and composed is absolutely necessary for successful spells and rituals, which is where mediation comes in. This technique helps you focus on what's really important for you by relaxing your mind and body, which is an added advantage. In this modern world, people think they need many more things in life than they actually do. Unfortunately, due to being overwhelmed by an abundance of possessions, they often lose focus on what they lack. As strange as this may sound initially, the only way to get what you want is to know exactly what you need. So, when you are visualizing your goals, be as specific as possible, so you can revere every little detail of what you can have.

In addition, if you want something in life, you need to treasure it even in the smallest amounts. This will help you imagine every aspect of a bigger picture you want to achieve eventually. You may also use other reminders of this ultimate goal, including writing it down in a journal, getting a picture of it and using it for small spells, and so on. Whether you want a particular item, a job, or a position in society, you will have to visualize it and make it manifest through your will. Make sure that every time you conjure the vision of your goal, you also attach positive feelings toward it. Spells can also help you do this, as saying your wishes aloud reaffirms the positivity of your actions, which is a sure way to manifest your desires. When choosing the spells or tools to work with, focus on the ones that work for you the best and those with which you are the most comfortable. After all, every individual has a different kind of natural energy, which may also vary in intensity in various stages of life. Therefore, spell manifestation – and the craft in general – will differ from one person to another. While you are casting a spell, your emotions at a particular moment can majorly influence the results! Also, each one of your thoughts has its own energy, which makes it possible for them to become a reality. If you have happy thoughts and do things that encourage you to have them, positivity will follow, and so will everything you need in life.

Chapter 3: Protection Magick 101: How to Handle the Nasties

Wondering why some people use witchcraft against people they perceive to be their opponents? Not all people have good intentions, and this is one of the major reasons why some people cast evil spells on other individuals. This chapter outlines the steps you can take to deal with the "nasties" or witches who direct their negativity at you.

These people can also cast dark spells and hexes or attack others physically. In some cases, this can be knowingly or unknowingly. This section of the book provides tips and techniques you can use to protect yourself against nasty people and spells. It also explains the value of the pentagram as a powerful symbol to shield yourself from the spirits that can affect you.

Impacts of Witchcraft

White magic is viewed as witchcraft since it involves using supernatural power for unselfish purposes. But, different forms of witchcraft, which do not bring something good but involve malicious practices aimed at destroying someone mentally, physically, or financially are usually referred to as black magic. The practice of bad witchcraft is not new, and witches often use the victim's items to cause them harm. The following are some of the symptoms that show the existence of evil spells in your life.

- The feeling of being surrounded by bad luck

- Being a victim of recurring accidents
- Feeling emotionally and mentally controlled
- Losing jobs
- Eccentric behavior
- Disturbances in sleeping and bad dreams
- Frequent financial losses and constant unhappiness
- Failing relationships
- Are you giving up on your family
- Headaches

Dealing with Nasty People

There is no universal remedy that victims can implement to deal with nasty people. However, there are numerous steps you can take to reduce or eliminate their impact. In this section, we will outline some of the measures that can help you overcome the challenges that may be related to witchcraft.

Avoid Conflicts

If you want to deal with people who behave in a nasty way toward you, try to avoid conflicts with them and remain unflappable. Confrontation or displaying aggressive behavior in retaliation can only worsen the situation. Some people get great pleasure from picking fights with almost everyone. The best way is to try to avoid conflict and maintain your cool. If you try to keep a positive attitude and show the other person that you are not pro-violence, they will not harm you. You could also try to show the other individual who treats you poorly some empathy and turn some nasty behavior into a friendly discussion. Instead of responding with anger, be empathetic and show concern. This action could be disarming since the perpetrator may soon realize that they are doing a bad thing.

Pray to God

God is the creator and ultimate power over all living things. Therefore, if you feel that others torment your spirit, pray directly to God and request everything you want from the highest authority there is. You can pray to God in the name of Jesus, the only begotten son who died for our sins. According to Christianity, Jesus has a lot of spiritual power, and those who practice evil things fear this name. Even the devil is scared of Jesus. If you feel you cannot pray through Jesus, call the name of God directly and ask other people to pray for you. There is power in group prayer, so ask your church members to pray for you.

Pray to God/Jesus/the Light for deliverance from the evil spirits. They will send some rescuing angels who can remove the dark spirits around you and provide light to fill your heart. Ask God to sever the darkness surrounding you, cut all ties with curses, and ask the angels to protect you from further attacks. The other important element to include in your prayers is to ask for wisdom and blessings while at the same time requesting your home to be cleansed. Avoid praying to the angels directly, but pray to God, the highest authority.

Overall, you must have faith in whatever you do and believe that your prayers will be answered. The placebo effect is powerful since positive thinking combined with belief can work wonders. Some people often view magical rituals as having psychologically therapeutic benefits. This view is shared by people who belong to different cultures. The proponents of this system make it clear that it is an addition to scientific medicine and rational thinking.

Spiritual Healers

Depending on your beliefs and religion, you can also seek help from spiritual healers, including white witches, Christian exorcists, Hindu Vedas, obeah therapists, energy cleansers, and Muslim Hakims. The people who perform spiritual rescue work can use charms to protect you against the spells. You can try to find help from people who use different techniques as long as you know that they can provide positive results. Make sure the person is gracious, wise, and kind. Avoid dealing with people who display signs of greed, pride, impatience, jealousy, hurtfulness, and a bruised ego.

The best rescue workers usually offer their services for free. Anyone who charges for their services can be seen as a sham. Money comes with horrible temptation, and it can turn spirit rescue workers ungracious and nasty. Requesting people to part with large sums of money to have the supposed curse cleansed is not good. Spreading conflict for the love of money is equally not right. Some healers will claim that the curse was caused by another innocent person, which is also a sign that you are dealing with an inexperienced healer. It is unacceptable for the healer to make ridiculous claims of being able to cure everything from witchcraft to other types of sickness.

Elevate Yourself

When you feel bad spells or nasties surround you, try to elevate your spiritual body. When your spirits are high, you will have a positive view of the universe which will strengthen you enough to overcome any weaknesses you may be facing. You can also move away from dangerous spiritual areas to safer places where there is light. Remember all the good things that can uplift your spirit and let them warm you. The other option you can consider is to recall all the moments that have filled you with joy and happiness to uplift your spirit.

Other activities you can do include walking in the park, listening to music, admiring the environment, or doing anything which soothes your spirit and mind. Try to do positive and constructive things that bring joy, hope, faith, compassion, and gratitude. Caring for someone is a great way of pushing your own problems aside, and you should not expect payment or reward when you choose this avenue. There is more happiness in giving than receiving. Deceitful and dark spirits are usually attracted to people who always want to receive things from other individuals.

However, suppose you have a true intention to give or help. In that case, you will attract benevolent spirits, which can go a long way toward lifting you out of the problems you are encountering. Let go of any worries, feelings of guilt, and fears. It does not help to dwell on the past since this will not help you change anything or reverse the situation.

Instead, let bygones be bygones and move on to start a better life rather than tie yourself to the past. Suppose you struggle with certain issues like addiction. In that case, it is crucial to seek deeper wisdom through prayer to overcome these challenges. Constant worries and tensions can drain you and present your enemies with openings to cause more harm.

Turn the Situation into an Opportunity

If you feel that someone is hell-bent on attacking you or causing you misery, turn the situation into an opportunity. Focus goodwill on the attacker and remember to bless them in whatever they do. Try to return a good reaction to your tormentor so that they can see that all that is happening is that good things are being made out of their bad behavior. If someone is doing bad things to you, turn it around into something good and see how this discourages the attackers. You will also enjoy lasting freedom and peace of mind if you can control your attackers. They are likely to develop positive attitudes that will help them to avoid bad things that can cause misery to other people.

Another important thing you can consider is to avoid taking the attack at face value or personally. Some attacks may seem frightening and threatening, but they may be nothing. The amount of fear you attach to some of these attacks can amplify them. You can consider fighting the attacker off together with your God, but don't expect Him to do everything for you. However, you must exercise caution and only consider this option for self-defense purposes. You should not curse the attacker but pray for their well-being. You must not pity the tormentor since this can give them room to connect with you. Make sure God is in it when you want the attacker to stay away from you.

Use Natural Herbs of Charms

You can improve your defense by including some raw herbs in your meals. For instance, raw garlic, onions, real mint, and fresh rosemary are believed to possess properties that can repel evil spells. Keeping a bouquet of flowers can also have a spiritual effect on you. Furthermore, consider walking in a sunlit garden. Natural foods will give you an energy boost, and the natural surroundings will uplift your spirit.

Use Your Psychic and Mental Shielding

The mind is the key component to fighting attacks. The main issue is that both bad and good influences can penetrate through to our wide-open minds. This means that you must exercise mind-control so that only you determine the things you want to keep and things you want to rid yourself of. You must try to shut the door on all unpleasant things, saving you from the burden of processing things that will not add any value to your life. Avoid negative voices or thoughts since they can contribute to mental illness. Some voices don't belong to God, so be careful about what you consume.

Another activity to be cautious about is to avoid prolonging communication with the spirits. The angels from God are busy, brisk, and they get straight to the point. If the spirits keep hanging around you, try to maintain your distance. Attempt to fill yourself with light and get rid of darkness – which is often associated with evil spells. The brightest light source comes from your Higher Power, so pray for it, and it will come into your heart. Try to visualize a sacred image when you sense a spiritual problem. For instance, picture Jesus healing the sick (if you are a Christian) and helping different individuals in need. This will help create power to overcome the spiritual challenges you may face.

Another simple method to overcome nasty spirits is to give yourself some time to relax. Allow your mind to rest and take deep breaths to help you refocus your attention on positive things instead of always seeing, sensing, and feeling dark connections. This may result from pressure in your mind, so aim to elevate your mind in the best way possible. Think about the good things that can happen to you and imagine the joy they will bring. Maintain your concentration on one thing and work on strategies to achieve your goals.

If you see something nasty, try to shut it out so that it doesn't distract you. Turn on the lights, and listen to music, which can help you think positively. Draw your mind away from negativity and focus on material sensations that will gradually remove the psychic world in your mind. You must have a positive goal in mind to prevent it from being vulnerable to the nasties if life seems purposeless. Your goals will help you remain focused on important things that can help you make a difference in life. Dark components will find it difficult to sway a busy and focused mind.

Moderate Your Alcohol Intake

Excessive alcohol consumption can be detrimental to your mental health and affect your overall well-being. If you pass out due to too much alcohol, you are likely to experience nasty spiritual influences that can ruin your life if you are not careful. The effects of alcoholism can also affect loved ones, especially children. Many people turn to alcohol to drown their sorrows, but this is not a solution. Try to avoid watching or reading unpleasant things.

Keep your mind occupied by positive things, and don't allow it to wander. If your mind is idle for a long period, it will become vulnerable and may become a target of attack. Try to be active most of the time to prevent mental attacks. Singing or performing other physical activities uplift your mind so that it does not wander. When you are in danger of attack while traveling, stop and find a comfortable place where you can rest. If you are weak, try to reinvigorate your energy level and get as much light and fresh air as possible.

Try to cut all your previous connections with darkness and focus on the brighter side of your life. When you are experiencing nasty thoughts, replace them with positive ones. Try to replace everything bad with spiritual images of God or other spiritual references that can give you strength and hope. Other issues like depression may require psychiatric help. Counseling or appropriate medication like anti-depressants can help you resist the influences that can affect your mind. Medicine can work if your challenge is caused by ailments like depression and anxiety.

Seek Counseling

You must avoid channeling the evil spirits but try to break any contact with the attacker. Seek counseling from someone who can elevate your spirit to realize the true love of God. If there is an evil spirit attached to you, it will be difficult to break away, so you need to be connected to a positive Higher Power to take strength from them. Some people have been deceived and told that God's light can destroy, but this is not true. These individuals need to be uplifted and need to be reminded about the happiness that comes with the light. It is essential to help the affected persons pray to God and seek the light.

Some spirits who attack people are not evil; they may be in pain, lost, or just confused. Do not communicate with the spirit, but try the option of sending it to the forest where it will not return to haunt you again. Try to close all connections with the spirits that you do not trust. These spirits can lead you astray if you keep in touch with them.

Know the Truth

There is often confusion about the spiritual world, and some nasty thoughts that people have may also be a figment of their imaginations. You need to develop the strength to resist them. You should know that negative and nasty thoughts are destructive, and they are not usually products of your mind. You must take the necessary steps to get rid of them and do not let other things influence you to be led astray by spirits.

Tell all the voices that may come into your ears saying that you deserve suffering to go away. A benevolent spirit god does not want us to suffer, so those voices may be from someone who does not wish you good things! Even if we sin against others, we can seek forgiveness, and He does not punish us for such things. When things are not going your way, you must never consider suicide as an option because it does not solve anything. Instead, the demons want you to commit suicide, which means you will have yielded to their demands if you terminate your life.

When you hear voices from the demons driving you to do things like attempting suicide, pray and ask God to rescue you from the temptation. You should have hope in life and try to overcome temptation. Another crucial thing you should do is not trust the spirits that may claim to be angels. Some angels may want you to depend on them for advice which is not recommended. God is the highest authority in which you should believe.

Pentagram

A pentagram is probably the oldest marking known to humankind, and it dates back to about 8,000 years ago. It is a transparent star that consists of five sides and is fraught with intrigue, a deep meaning, and mystery. Wiccans use the pentagram, and they attach five different meanings to the pentagram points, including fire, earth, water, sky, and spirit. The spirit occupies the top position, and it is the most important. In some cultures, the pentagram is used for evil purposes, while others use it to ward off spells and other bad things.

Witchcraft is common and in different places, driven by jealousy and other undesirable elements. Some people can do nasty things designed to cause spiritual and physical harm. However, there are various things you can do to deal with nasties. With these tips, you can overcome the challenges likely to be caused by others. In whatever you do, you must remember that God is the highest authority.

Chapter 4: Candle Magick for the White Witch

After gaining a little more insight into the events that shaped the makings of modern white magic and understanding its basic principles, it's now time to explore candle magick. Being one of the most elemental forms of magic, candle magick has been used in several cultures throughout centuries. This is one of the best ways to convey your intentions – because using candles during rituals and spellcasting is recommended particularly for new spiritual seekers. It's also beneficial for anyone looking to forge a deeper connection with natural magic. This chapter contains everything you need to know about candle magick, including its nature and possible uses. You will also learn why stating clear and positive intentions is crucial for a successful spell or ritual involving candles.

Candle Magick Basics

Before opting for Candle magick in your craft, firstly, you need to understand how this form of magic helps convey and manifest your intent. Candle magick is a form of sympathetic magic. You are essentially using the candle to represent an item or a person you wish to influence. There are two ways to perform sympathetic magic: similarity or contact. The first method relies on using an object and simply producing the desired effect by imitating the practitioner's will. The second one refers to the use of objects which had previous contact with the item or person in question, which further improves the chances of influencing them successfully. Candle magick clearly belongs to the first category as the candles you use don't have to come in contact with the person or item you are trying to influence. You may use other symbols that represent your target, along with candles.

The concept of sympathetic magic plays a huge role when using candles for spells and rituals. Using this approach, you can influence someone's life through something that represents them, which, in this case, is a candle. This core principle makes candle magic easy and one of the most popular Wiccan practices.

Like many modern magical practices, Wiccan white magic also relies heavily on connections between the world of magic and items without magical powers. These items, albeit non-magical in essence, represent a tie to the spiritual world and are therefore capable of carrying correspondence between spirits and the practitioner. Besides candles, crystals, herbs, and other symbols are also used for these purposes.

Due to the modern approach to white magic, a witch must understand the psychological force at play while using sympathetic candle magick. As mentioned in a previous chapter, the Craft is based on manifesting one's will and making positive changes in how you use it. Through sympathetic magic, a white witch can enter into the space of their target and make changes necessary through its essence, rather than just to your own focus. Candles help you focus on creating an affinity to urge your natural power into this foreign state of existence, whether it's a living being or an item. Naturally, living beings have a stronger essence, making them much easier to influence.

From prehistoric paintings to fire magic, people have successfully used sympathy to connect with other spirits. This means its benefits have been proven repeatedly, from primitive to modern societies. Naturally, through candle magic, you are affecting the destiny of your target, be it a living being, a concept, or an object. For this reason, before you delve into practicing candle magic, you must understand how to do it safely. Learning how to use your consciousness to influence your target doesn't mean that you are equipped with enough knowledge to make the correct changes.

Unlike any other creatures of nature, humans have a fully developed consciousness, enabling them to develop into a higher state of being. If you decide to embark on the journey to becoming a white witch, it will also be possible due to your consciousness. It allows you to believe in magic and establish a connection via magical or non-magical elements - which in this case is *the candle*. Besides the aforementioned psychological factor, sympathetic candle magic also has a cultural aspect, particularly if you are practicing within a coven. While modern covens don't work under the same rigorous concept as indigenous tribes would practice magick as recently as a hundred years ago, they are similar rituals. Since members of a coven often work toward common goals, they can safely influence natural forces to affect each other's lives. They can also use candle magic to defend against dark spells, as long as they don't intend to harm their target.

Of course, this doesn't mean that solitary practitioners cannot use candle magic. However, unless you are only using your Craft to help fellow witches, you will need to establish a few boundaries. Using candle magic can be the perfect way to learn everything you need about connecting with others, spreading love, and obtaining prosperity. However, your approach has to remain benevolent at all times. You must remember one of the cardinal rules of Wicca - you can achieve any magical goal in life as long as it serves the common good. Once that is accomplished, you can expect to receive your own reward.

How to Start Practicing Candle Magick

When your chosen spell requires candle magick, it's very important you check how you will use your candle and the spell. From determining a clear intent to the color of the candle, every little detail plays a role in determining the success of the spell. In some spells, even the placement of the candles is predetermined, and you must ensure you light the right candle in the right place on your altar. Remember, candle magick is a sacred ritual that can only enlighten your practice if you are willing to put in the effort. Doing so will help make a positive change in your life and the world. As you begin experiencing the positive changes in your mood and mindset, you become even more productive in your craft, enabling you to affect natural energy even more.

Furthermore, each part of a candle represents an element of nature. When you are lighting a candle, you are activating the Fire. As the flame of the burning candle purifies the power you are harnessing. This represents the start of the ritual, which will bring you or your target the desired change. As the candle burns, the hot wax melts, and as it drips down, it mimics the properties of Water. Now, your intent is out and ready to make the connection. The pooling wax at the bottom of a candle indicates that you have successfully connected to nature through Earth. And finally, as the candle is finished, it emits smoke signifying that the change is in the Air, which will soon happen.

When it comes to choosing the color of your candle, the idea is to attract the type of energy your spell or ritual requires. Different colors symbolize different elements of nature, which come with various powers. The candle flame is also crucial for a white witch, and it's often required for healing spells. The power of the flame is also dependent on the type and color of the candle you choose, so it's another very powerful reason to be careful with this step. Make sure you consider your intent first and then the circumstances under which you plan to use the candle.

After learning how to control the function of a candle in your spells, you may move on to different dressing techniques and even learn to combine the use of candles with oils. Anointing can enhance the power of candle magick, but only if it's done safely. For a beginner, even a basic form of candle magic can add an additional boost of energy that you need to advance your craft. If you practice candle magic over time, you have a tool that helps you visualize your intent over and over again. You have the opportunity to observe your magic working in real-time, which promotes the positive attitude you need to cherish as a white witch.

There are many ways to approach candle magic, and you will have to find what works best for you. Below, you will find a step-by-step guide to get you started, but you can personalize it to your liking. Once you establish what makes you focus more, feel free to implement it into your practices and use it as often as you can. This way, you will have a well-established process for charging your ritual, and your spells will work every time.

1. Setting Your Intention

The first step when working with candle magick is determining what exactly it is that you want to accomplish. You may use a candle to attract good energy, banish bad energy, or gain protection from dark spells. To charge your energy successfully, you must get clear about your intentions from the start. If you have trouble focusing on your intent, meditation exercises can help you to be concise. You can also write your intention down on a piece of paper and keep it near the candle while it's burning. Another option would be to carve the message into the candle to help channel your energy.

2. Choosing Candles

The size of your candle can determine how long the spell will last. If you want your magick to last for days or weeks, you will need to choose a candle that will burn for a longer period. On the other hand, if the spell only needs to last for a couple of hours, you may use a thinner candle. When it comes to choosing colors, the choice becomes a little trickier. Each color represents specific energy, so your intent will determine your choice:

- **White:** Works best to manifest the changes you want to make and attract positive energy
- **Black:** Particularly useful for banishing the negativity around your target and repelling harmful spells
- **Red**: Great for bringing passion into one's life and boosting their sexual energy
- **Pink:** Promotes self-acceptance as well as love and compassion toward others
- **Orange:** Vitalizes the flow of creative juices in body and mind, which manifests in productivity in magick
- **Yellow**: Provides inspiration for your practice and other areas of life
- **Green:** Helps attract material possessions and facilitates creating wealth in a healthy way
- **Blue**: Perfect for spells that aim to reestablish harmony and health within the mind and body

- **Purple**: Mainly used to establish a strong spiritual connection with one's guide

3. Picking Your Dressing

If you want to enhance candle magick, you need to dress the candle in oils or herbs. For beginners, it's a good idea to start a simple dressing like olive oil, which you probably have at home. Once you get the hang of it, you may move on to specific blends designed to work with different types of magic. Nowadays, these oils are widely available in esoteric shops and online. Ideally, the herbs should also match your magick. Some of the most commonly used herbs are eucalyptus (for healing), rose (for love), or mugwort (for spiritual connection).

4. Carving Your Candle

If you have opted for solidifying your intention by carving it into the candle, you can do that at this stage. For starters, just write it down simply on the candle with a pen. As you learn more about symbols, you can also begin to carve those into your candles. Whichever method you choose, you must start the carving from the top of the candle and work your way toward the middle. When you get there, move on to the bottom, and curve upwards to the middle until you reach the point where you stopped before.

5. Anointing Your Magic

Once you have finished carving your intention into your candle, coat the candle's surface with the oil or herb dressing of your choice. First, cover your hands in the oil, then move it on your candle in the same pattern as you did the carving. This works well for manifesting, while you must move in the opposite direction for banishing. Start from the middle to the top and then from the middle to the bottom. Repeat the same process with the herbs, too, while making sure you distribute them on the candles on every side. Some people choose to seal the herbs and oils by dripping the wax from another candle on top of it. Be careful with your herbs - don't let the flame near them, or otherwise, they may catch on fire, along with the oils.

6. Creating Spells and Rituals

Now it's time to start creating the actual spell or ritual or spell you intend to enact. How you do this depends on your usual craft and your experience levels. If you need help focusing on the change you wish to manifest, you can use some relaxation techniques before you get to crafting. Try meditation, taking a relaxing bath, cleansing with herbs and incense, or whatever method calms your mind. Make sure you are peaceful and won't be disturbed during your work with candle magick. You may do this at your altar or inside the circle you have cast for this purpose. Once you feel ready to state your intent clearly, light a candle and focus on whatever you are trying to accomplish for a couple of minutes. If it's a short-term spell, and you are using a thinner candle, you may let it burn until it's finished. Thicker candles for long-term spells should be put out with a snuffer after a couple of hours and relit every day afterward for the period the spell needs to last. Don't forget to thank nature for helping you out with the spell after it's completed.

7. Disposing of Candle Wax

You can either throw away the used wax or keep it in a jar and remake it into candles for future use. Whether you decide to keep it or not will depend on your preferences, as well as on the magick you have used it for. Some candle spell combinations have specific purposes, and reusing them just wouldn't feel right. Others may fill you with positive energy and can be used multiple times, particularly when you work hard to manifest something. Using the same energy will make it easier for your mind and body to focus every time you revisit the intention.

Final Advice

When you are using candle magic to represent another person via a spell or ritual, you need to make sure you gain their consent, and for multiple reasons. For one, no matter how good your intentions are, you can't just decide what works for someone else's benefit and what doesn't. If you see that someone is in trouble, you may offer your help and ask them for their consent to represent them. However, you cannot assume they would consent, even if they know you well. They may not have as deep an understanding of the benefits of white magic as a practitioner does. The only exception from this rule is the use of healing spells, but only if you are casting them for entirely selfless reasons. Suppose your only goal is to help someone without expecting anything in return. There won't be a risk of the spell returning in the form of harmful energy in that case. While a binding spell that prevents someone from hurting others may also be considered a selfless act, it often results in harming the person upon whom the spell is cast, so it's best to avoid it.

Another crucial reason for asking for a person's consent before representing them in candle magic is to avoid the violation of their privacy. This is considered a malicious act, which, as you already know, belongs to the realms of black magic. Even if you try to manipulate the circumstances in a way for them to gain an advantage from something they aren't aware of, this may hurt them in the long run. And most importantly, it will definitely harm you. Casting a spell for reasons that aren't pure creates a lot of negative energy, which, if you send it out there, may very well come back to your threefold. If your request for consent for a spell with good intentions gets denied, and you still decide to go ahead with casting it, this is also considered black magic. Again, this may yield undesirable results, if not for the target, then for you. It's best to stay away from any type of manipulation when representing another person and avoid getting hit by the negative side of the Wiccan law of three. Remember, your goal is to work with nature, not against it – and misusing natural forces either directly or indirectly could seriously backfire.

Chapter 5: Magical Blessing Rituals to Spread Your Light

White magic spells used for selfless purposes are simply one of the ways you can use white magic. However, it's believed only those born with supernatural powers can practice white magic or cast these spells. For people who believe in magic, white magic is the opposite of dark or black magic, which is the evil form of magic used to satisfy the malevolent intentions of its practitioners. White magic is also referred to as Natural Magic due to its connection with Agnosticism or nature veneration. Blessing rituals are a type of spell used in white magic and include love, attraction, career, and job spells. Let's delve right into the dynamics of the different white magic blessing rituals and show you how you can use them to spread positivity.

White Magic Spells and How They Work

When you hear the term white magic, you should think of the type of magic that is practiced with good intentions. Many people claim that the use of magic spells is one of the most powerful tools, and we're about to find out why. For any person to cast a magical spell or engage in a magical ritual, they need to learn to master most of the white magic principles and fundamentals. Yet, it's not just about magic. The process can be a life-long journey of self-discovery that consumes all of your desire and patience.

Many people wonder if they can practice spells and magical rituals at home. Practicing at home requires precautions and special preparations, including finding a sacred and safe space where you can quietly engage in your divine practices. You can easily practice white magic at home if you have enough space; you don't necessarily have to be a master of witchcraft or a member of a Coven. You can also seek the help of professionals to help you practice a confidence-boosting magical ritual that gets you closer to your desires. The best thing about white magic rituals and spells is that they can be used to enhance and bring positivity to any aspect of your life.

They also involve a great amount of self-development where you reflect internally while listening to your intuition. To effectively work with white magic spells, you have to align with your inner voices and determine the core desires of your inner self. It's all about letting your higher self take over and being mindful enough to recognize the signs.

The Types of Magical Spells and Rituals in White Magic

There are many types of spells and special practices that you can try if you're new to white magic. Here are a few.

Love Spells

Many categories revolve around the different struggles or issues people experience with love when it comes to love spells. For example, many spells help strengthen or improve romantic relationships, fall in love with a particular person, increase attractiveness, recover one's ex-lover, forget or get over someone, compromise or reconcile in relationships, and revive the love between couples, and avoid infidelity. Love spells target the various struggles and troubles of the heart, and they can definitely help you make a difference. You can easily practice these spells at home if your intentions are good enough. Just make sure you get help from a professional to ensure you don't allow any negative impacts to occur due to the love spell.

Wealth or Fortune Spells

Fortune spells focus on the tangible and intangible gifts we're blessed with in life. They're used to improve one's financial status and bring more luck and prosperity. These spells are very helpful for making rich and positive changes to your destiny. There are many variations of these spells, such as paying debts, winning the lottery, and attracting more money. There are also various ways these spells can be cast to bring more fortune into your life. There are also many spellcaster rituals that help clear negativity from your aura to attract better fortuity. They work on blessing three areas of your life: money, home, and work.

Health Spells

This group of rituals and spells is used to improve mental and physical wellness. These spells work using the same concept in that they clear out negative energy, heal physical pains and aches, and harmonize the aura. Health spells and rituals are simply good for your body and soul, and they are necessary if your goal is to grow spiritually and develop your mental skills.

Blessing Spells

Blessing spells are similar to fortune spells. They bring more luck, positivity, and joy into your life. There are a lot of different forms of blessing spells, as well as white magic practices focusing on blessing people, animals, items, and various spiritual concepts. The dynamic of this category of spells is based on dispersing negativity and encouraging more grace into one's life. Blessing spells, like many other white magic spells, can be practiced at home by people who are not experienced in witchcraft.

Energy Clearing Home Makeover Rituals

Energy clearing home makeover rituals rely on the idea of redecorating and cleaning the home to balance and improve its energy. The intention is to dispose of negative energy and replace it with grace and abundance or, in other words, positivity. This is based on three main focuses, cleansing the energy, decluttering the space, and creating a peaceful and good-natured environment where negative energy is not welcomed. White magic involves the use of witchcraft to bring about a sense of joy and happiness to every room within the home, along with enhancing the ambiance and adding harmony to the mix. Each of the six fundamental elements in the house energy-clearing process can be used as a stand-alone special spell for every part of your house. Here are the steps used to cast blessing spells for restoring a home's energy.

Expelling

This step is all about clearing your home's old energy and replacing it with new refreshing energy. You have to make sure you physically clean the space before inviting new energy into the house. The recommended technique focuses on charging your cleaning supplies. This is a spiritual process where you hold the supplies, meditate with them, think about previous chore-related arguments you have had while using the supplies and equipment thoroughly, and clean out these thoughts and related negative emotions along with the cleaning equipment.

A very important step in the process is creating a mantra that helps to clear the negative energy. This should be something like, "I wish to replace this place's negative energy with my balanced and rich energy." Always aim to finish off your mantra with clear and honest communication.

Manifesting

A great way to manifest happiness and summon good vibes is to set up an altar for your door keys. If you haven't heard of an altar before, it was defined previously as an unusual and raised structure on which sacrifices are offered. It is also used as a place to burn incense in worship. To recap, here's how you can decorate your altar. Start by placing an altar bell as a divination symbol or tool, and use rose quartz to embellish the corners of the table and strengthen the love energy in the house. You can also place photo frames and little glass bowls for the keys to complete the aesthetic.

While holding the new keys, make sure you practice some manifestations such as visualizing your home's door opening to a myriad of fulfillment, ease, abundance, or self-love. Think of any form of blessing you want your home to manifest and make it come true by mastering your intentions. It's all about the internal ambition you put into the process.

Harmony

A more complex study is held to coordinate and balance the energy inside your home. You'll need to harmonize the space you have at home and summon a great deal of positivity so that every family member is spiritually satisfied. This is why you'll need to turn to your birth chart and examine astrological compatibility. Look for your moon sign. While many people already know their sun sign, the moon sign can provide very helpful home-related information. You can use these insights to harmonize energies accordingly and bring peace into your home.

Comfort

Many white magic rituals work to facilitate more comfort and solace within your home. The specific spell or ritual used for this purpose can be practiced using a few simple ingredients such as comfortable clothes, orange candles, and cookie dough. Cookie dough, in particular, is used by realtors as an innovative idea to create a warm and inviting ambiance in any open house. You may not be a baking person, or you may simply not enjoy the sweet scent of homemade cookies. If that sounds like you, there's another recipe for home blessing. You can light up a few orange-scented candles to create a refreshing and invigorating aroma to fill your space, or you can peel and slice some oranges and put them in a pot of boiling water along with vanilla extract and cinnamon sticks. The mixture's steam will let out a delightful sugary scent that brings all the peaceful energy into your dwelling.

Balance

Balance is when you satisfy and match the energy existing in your home. This requires studying a little about earth elements to figure out how to represent each energy. If you're living with roommates, you'll need to match their energy with an earth element to create harmony and enhance your home's ambiance and mood. Use a spell that can bring peace and transparency. For example, you'll need to represent every roommate or family member with two elements to identify their energy type. The four elements are Fire, Water, Air, and Earth. To represent these elements, you'll need scented candles to symbolize fire and other symbolic items such as seashells to represent water, incense to represent air, and crystals to represent the earth. Remember that you'll also need two of each item to manifest balance and bring equilibrium. This will balance the energies in your house and create peaceful relationships between the people living with you.

When setting up these aesthetic additions, make sure you meditate about past living situations and identify the memories that don't sit well in your head. It's very important to let go of any negative emotions you're keeping toward any particular past event. The goal is to observe and not to react or dwell on it, so make sure you align with your inner voices when bringing balance into your home aura. It will help with the efficiency of your blessing ritual and keep you on track with your goals. Focus on what you're leaving behind and what you're trying to manifest.

Protection

Now that you have tackled all of the important aspects of your home-blessing spell or ritual, the only thing left to do is to claim your space. This is very easy – simply say it out loud. Seriously, stand in any quiet space in your home and announce your intentions out loud. Make it clear to yourself and the universe that this place belongs to you and your roommates or family members and that you're not welcoming any negative energy or malicious intentions. You can also increase security and protect your dwelling place by buying crystals and placing them around the house. Obsidian and black tourmaline are ideal for protection spells.

Another element that is cheap and easily accessible is salt. It's one of the most efficient and super-sacred white magic protection tools. It will keep you safe and balanced as long as you follow the right rituals. You can sprinkle a few grains of salt in every corner of your house, or you can draw a circle of salt around your building for optimum protection.

By initiating these good-natured gestures, you build a powerful magical ritual that harmonizes your home and protects you. By now, you should already understand how the whole process relies on your deep intentional desires and how you resonate with your inner self. It can be a long journey, and that requires a lot of patience and energy, but you'll get there. Just focus on being mindful of your spiritual tendencies to speed up the awakening process – expand your aura to the point it shields your home. In fact, dedicating your time to learning how to practice magical rituals and cast spells will help you develop healthier lines of communication and provide you with deeper bonding experiences.

The reason that these spells or magic work in the first place is because of the amount of energy you dedicate to believing and learning. So even if we're talking from a more scientific point of view, the law of attraction comes into place, and you'll manage to attract the positive things which match your positive vibes. The more you practice magic, the more you'll feel aligned with your goals and the more control you'll have over your space.

The Importance of Meditation for White Magic

Meditation is considered magic due to the numerous positive health effects it offers and the emotional relief it promotes to those who meditate. Meditation is one of the best treatments for anxiety and stress. It helps calm your thoughts and gives you an expanded external perspective to stay mindful of your feelings. It's like therapy, but easier, cheaper, and much more effective when you get it right.

According to recent studies, many emotional and physiological changes occur when you meditate. The metabolism in our body slows down when we meditate to let us relax and give our internal functions a break they desperately need. Your body organs literally relax when you meditate, which means you obtain more strength and refresh your body. Meditation also works on cleansing the mind and allowing healthier new perspectives. When you clear out old energy, you make room for new adjustments to your consciousness and give yourself the chance to grow and heal. It's all about breaking old patterns and habits.

This is why meditation is like a magical doorway to the wonderful experience of spirituality and practicing good-natured magic. It's also one of the most peaceful and grounding techniques to start this divine journey and focus on your mental health. Meditation helps us switch our consciousness and become more aware of our surroundings and the connections with those around us. You'll gradually grasp the main teachings and realize that we are all one. This is what happens when you align with your higher awareness. The practice itself brings more positivity into your reality and helps to keep your head and body in the right healthy place, which means you take care of both your physical and mental health.

Gratitude and White Magic

Gratitude is a key factor in white magic, as is mindfulness. You can't completely love yourself and align with your inner voices if you don't practice gratitude. You can't find happiness if you're not living in the moment and finding satisfaction in what you have. Keep in mind that gratitude is very similar to forgiveness. If you can't forgive yourself, you can't forgive others, and you most definitely can't find internal peace. You have to forgive and let go for your own benefit. You also need to work on being grateful for what you have so that you can truly find what you're looking for. It's a universal paradox, but you can really rely on the rewards. Just focus on creating your happiness through taking care of yourself and finding satisfaction in what you already have. It's your own reality, and you can choose to make it a positive one.

Chapter 6: The White Witch's Apothecary

While a white witch usually relies on her own ability to harness nature's energy, the elements she uses can significantly enhance her magick. The ingredients you keep in your apothecary are fundamental for successful spellcasting - as well as most rituals you might perform. This chapter is dedicated to all the herbs and oils you can take advantage of in your craft. Whether you decide to grow the herbs and make the ingredients of your spell at home or buy them prepared, you will need to be aware of their inordinate powers. You will also be given a few examples of spells for prosperity, in which you can use the herbs and oils from your apothecary.

Herbs Every White Witch Needs to Have in Their Apothecary

From helping you focus on your intent to empowering healing spells, plants have so many magical properties! Keep in mind that it may take some time to learn how to use them properly and before you see the desired results, but this is one of the greatest lessons of this craft. It teaches you patience and the benefits of working for your goals. If you have the space for it, you may want to keep your own herb garden. It doesn't even have to be a large one. Even a few pots on the balcony or kitchen will do if you grow the right plants. If you don't have space, you can get most herbs, fresh or dried, from the local supermarket or health shop. Below you will find a list of herbs with magical properties you can harness in your craft.

Calendula

This plant has been long revered for its ability to promote emotional well-being. Not only do its flowers smell and look pleasant, but you can use them to create a relaxing environment, necessary for focusing on your intent during spellwork. Calendula fares well when planted in small pots, so it's easy to keep even if you have limited space. You can keep the dried flowers with you on a stressful day or use them to dress a candle during a spell that's meant to alleviate anxiety.

Patchouli

If you feel that you could use some more luck in certain aspects of your life, patchouli can help you get it. Plant it in your garden or balcony or get it from the store, and luck will already begin to follow you. Naturally, you can use it in spells and rituals, as well as to make sure that luck favors you in a particularly important project or event.

Lemongrass

While it's mostly known as an aromatic herb used in the kitchen, lemongrass has amazing magical abilities. This herb works wonders for emotional healing and is used in a spell. It can chase away many sleepless nights caused by anxiety or depression. It's also said to alleviate physical pain, whether caused by a mental illness or a physical one. The person who needs it can keep lemongrass with them during hard times -or you can infuse its powers through candle magic, and it will relieve the symptoms.

Sage

If you or your target deals with negative energy around them, sage can help dissipate it. Whether they come from a black witch's spell or a hostile person, all dark intentions can easily be deflected with the proper spells and herbs like sage. For best results, use dried sage mixed with sea salt, which also helps banish dark thoughts. Cast a circle by sprinkling the mixture on the floor before spellcasting. If you want to cleanse your home from bad vibes, you may spread the mixture around it in a clockwise motion or plant sage in various corners of the house.

Lavender

Due to its ability to provide emotional relief and prosperity, lavender is a herb that has many uses in magick practices. Depending on your intention, you may combine this herb with spells for calming nerves, spiritual cleansing, restoring balance, or achieving specific goals. For the first two purposes, put dried lavender in a small sachet or container along with rose quartz crystal and keep it with you while sleeping. You may also use this plant for prosperity spells, either dried or as an oil.

Mint

Yet another plant that you can grow in your own home – mint is perfect to attract financial prosperity. If you feel that you just need a little luck getting money, mix crushed mint leaves with an oil that has similar properties, and dress a green candle with the mixture. Or, if you want to keep luck on your side for a longer period of time, plant mint in a small spot, and if you care for it properly, you will keep achieving as much wealth as you need.

Dandelion

Believe it or not, even this plant that's often dubbed as a common weed also has some pretty amazing magical abilities. If you ever wondered how dandelions could just sprout anywhere, now you know where this tenacity comes from. Live plants are great for meditating and harnessing the power of nature. If you have a particularly stressful event ahead of you, you may use dried dandelion parts in your spellwork. It will provide you with the motivation you need to get over the huddle.

Honeysuckle

The best way for a white witch to use her gifts to strengthen love and personal connection is to use the natural energy provided by herbs like honeysuckle. Not only can its aroma put anyone in a more generous and caring mood, but you can also use this plant to find out what someone's true desires are. Honeysuckle is a very sturdy plant, and if you can, keep it a pot as well. If you keep it outside, cut off its leaves during the winter, dry them and add them to your apothecary.

Nettle

Nettle is another great plant to have in your apothecary for defense against negative energy. You may keep it potted as well near your doorstep, so it can effectively block any malicious influence that's trying to enter your home. Nettle is also useful in spells when you are trying to conjure privacy during an emotionally trying period.

Garlic

It's common knowledge that garlic has special healing properties when used in meal preparation. You may have also heard about its ability to ward off malicious spirits as well. However, garlic can also be used for other magical purposes, including preventing jealousy. Keep a bunch of garlic in your kitchen to ensure that whoever enters will not succumb to jealousy.

Thyme

If you or your target is overcome with grief, thyme can help relieve the pain. The person who is in mourning should wear a sprig of thyme to ease the process. Or you may use a spell using dried thyme on them (with their consent) to help them to recover. Keeping this plant in your apothecary or in a pot will ensure that you will always have a helping hand with handling grief.

Rosemary

Rosemary is known for its ability to enhance mental and emotional clarity, making it perfect if you struggle to focus on your intention. In addition, if you need a little push to make an important decision, this fragrant plant will provide it for you. Hang a spring of fresh rosemary in your window overnight, and come morning, it will settle any uneasiness you have felt due to the decision.

Basil

Basil is another plant that enhances the body's healing properties, but that's not its best property. It's also great for gaining prosperity, healing emotional scars, and attaining peace and harmony. Basil planted in a pot works best to attract wealth whereas, soaked in water, it will provide the water with healing properties, which you may apply on a person or object representing them.

When it comes to charging your spellcasting ingredients with natural energy, this is easy to do, particularly by using the herbs you grow yourself. Plants thrive from the elements like sun and water, so all you need to do is provide these in the appropriate amounts, and they will be filled with the magical powers of nature. Even if you have one or more windowsills to keep your pots on, as long as it faces in a direction allowing the plant to get plenty of natural light, it will help charge your herbs. Make sure you keep the plants at appropriate temperatures and don't overwater them, especially when kept indoors. It's best to water plants in the morning so they can slowly soak up the power from the earth as the water evaporates throughout the day. Store-bought herbs, whether fresh or dry, can be given an extra boost of magical energy with the help of a crystal. Or you can charge them in a similar manner as is done for oils, which will be described later on in this chapter.

Magical Oils to Keep in Your Apothecary

Essential oils are widely popular through their use in traditional aromatherapy. From relieving a simple headache to alleviating the symptoms of anxiety and physical conditions, they seem to help with many maladies. Many people don't know is that all the abilities these oils possess are rooted in the magical energy contained within them. For this reason, essential oils are also necessary ingredients that every white witch should keep in their apothecary. Whether used in cleansing baths, vapors, or ointments, these magical oils can enrich your practice by strengthening your mind. This, in turn, is making it easier to manifest your intent. Another way to use essential oils is by anointing your tools with them. There are many ways to enhance an act of magick with essential oil, from empowering crystals, talismans, and candles.

Most essential oils are derived from magical herbs – some of them are even extracted from the same ones you may also use in dried form. Since these oils contain the concentrated essence of these plants, their power will be greater as well. While there are also essential oils that aren't made of natural ingredients, these should never be used by a white witch. Remember, plants are parts of nature, and your aim is to harness the plant's magical powers. Without the element of nature, you have no use for oil.

Essential oils are also considered to have magical properties simply due to their ability to affect one's mind through their fragrance. Most of them have a captivating scent that leaves a huge impact on human consciousness. First, it penetrates your subconscious mind, leaving behind a cluster of positive impressions. Next time you smell the same fragrance, your mind will automatically associate it with good memories, changing your mood instantly for the better.

Here are the most common types of essential oils that a white witch needs to have in her apothecary:

- **Peppermint:** With its invigorating scent, this oil is guaranteed to wake up your senses and provide you with the clarity you need for your practices. It also has healing properties and may be used in cleansing spells.

- **Lemon:** Like the previous herb, the aroma of lemon oil is also used to promote mental and emotional clarity. Using it regularly could make sure you stay healthy and full of positive energy for your magick.
- **Eucalyptus:** This oil has the best of both worlds. It can calm your senses enough to help you relax, but without dulling them too much. Furthermore, eucalyptus oil can be great for restoring emotional balance.
- **Chamomile:** If you need spiritual guidance during your magic, you can use chamomile oil to raise your awareness during meditation. It may also relieve anxiety and calm overly sensitive nerves.
- **Clove:** This oil has a particularly aromatic scent that can have an enormous impact on your magick. You can use it to cleanse and energize your body and mind, and therefore your powers as well. In some rituals, clove oil may ward off malicious intent.
- **Frankincense:** With its comforting smell, frankincense oil is one of the best tools for a successful manifestation. It's particularly helpful in focusing your powers to invoke protection and energy purification.

While all these oils can enrich your practice in certain forms, some of them have very distinctive properties. The ones you use in each spell or ritual will be determined when you have set your intent.

Charging Your Oils

Apart from gaining an understanding of their individual qualities, using essential oils requires you to charge their energy first. This will ensure they not only suit your needs – but also provide you with the desired results. Charging refers to the process during which oil is given a specific purpose. It's the final step in preparing them that's aimed to ensure that the oils are ready to use in the spell or ritual you need them for. It may sound like a complicated process but charging essential oils is actually a simple act of magick. Magical oils are designed to be carriers of the natural powers they were created from, which means they will just as easily soak up your light too. If you made the oil yourself, it already has some of your essences, which makes charging it with more of your power will be that much easier.

When it comes to ready-made oils, it's a good idea to cleanse them, as well, before charging them. They could have picked up negative energy until they found their way to your apothecary, and they will be helpful if used in that state.

Charging essential oils can be done in several different ways, but each one of them has one thing in common. Since their purpose is to reconnect the particular oil with nature, all charging processes require leaving the oil to sit undisturbed in one spot for a period.

Some of the common choices for charging essential oils are:

- **With Moonlight:** If you are planning to use your oil to enhance a spell intended to forge loving connections, or evoke empathy and compassion, leaving it under the full moon will work wonders on it. For the best results, pour the oil into a glass jar and place it under direct moonlight so the moon can penetrate it and infuse it with its powers. Leaving it for a couple of nights undisturbed created a very potent tool for your practices.

- **Underground:** There is no better way to supercharge your oil with nature's power than to burn it under the earth. This recreated the elemental connection the herbs the oils were made from had with the ground. You don't have to put it too deeply. You only need to cover it with a thin layer of topsoil. Doing this at noon when the earth is the warmest will ensure that the oils are infused with all the healing and protective properties nature can provide us.

- **Submerged in Water:** Due to its tricky nature, charging oils under water is less popular. However, this method can also act as a cleansing ritual that helps disperse any negative energy from it. If you cannot find a safe way to submerge the oil in a pool or small pond, you can collect rainwater and place the oil in it.

Whichever method you choose to charge your oils, you must finalize the process by infusing them with your intention. Each day, return to the spot where you have left the oil and recite the intent over it. Once you feel that enough days have passed and the oil is sufficiently imbued with the notion you are trying to manifest, bring it back to your apothecary.

Prosperity Spells

One of the easiest ways to employ herbs and essential oils from your apothecary is through prosperity spells. Here are some spells that will help you attract wealth.

Candle Magick Money Spell

Gather a thick green or white candle and your favorite oil and herbs, and make sure you feel energized before you start casting the spell. You can dance, clean, or do anything else that increases blood flow and gets your magical energy flowing more freely through your body. Once you feel it, anoint your candle by carving your name into it and covering it with the oil and herbs. Light the candle while calling the money toward you.

Try to visualize it as if it is right in front of you, and think about what you would do with it. Having done that, repeat the following spell three times:

"Money, money, come to me
In abundance, three times three
May I be enriched in the best of ways
Harming none, on its way.
This I accept, so mote it be
Give me money, three times three."

Start this ritual at the new moon, and light the candle every day after that until it burns completely.

A Spell for Acquiring the Desired Position

Gather a gold pen, a piece of green paper, three mint leaves, a teaspoon of dried sage, and a gold or silver candle. Draw a symbol of prosperity of your choice on the paper, then write either the name of the position you want or the word job. If you do the latter, add a couple of words around it that describe what kind of job you want – the desired salary and everything you can think of about it.

Place the herbs on top of the symbols and light the candle saying the following:

"Goddess Morrigan, hear my plea
Send me a job to help my needs
Give me a job that I will love

I send this message to you above."

Let the candle burn down completely, and when it's finished, open a window, and blow the herbs from the paper into the air.

Salt Bath at Full Moon

Just as you can charge your magical items with the light of a full moon, you can also do this with your own body. Once you feel that you have gained enough strength from the moon, take a quick shower, followed up with a salt bath. Magnesium salt works best for this purpose, but you can use sea salt as well. Soaking in it for at least half an hour will ensure that your mind relaxes, so you can focus on manifesting your goals at your next spellcasting or ritual. This will leave more room for the energy of the full moon to infuse your mind and release it from any block preventing you from reaching your target.

Chapter 7: Heal Thyself…Like White Witches Do

Before you can share your light with others, you must make sure you have enough to share yourself. Sometimes you need to step back from helping other people, and check in with yourself, and do the necessary healing before you can carry on with your work of healing others. You must understand that your ability to survive the worst gives you the foundation from which you are able to share your strength. In fact, many new witches are initiated into this path when looking for spiritual healing. This doesn't mean that you have to be in a perfect physical or mental state to become a productive witch, but you must acknowledge your own problems and heal them first. Life has its ups and downs, and sometimes pain is inevitable. However, the sooner you can recover, the more your powers will grow.

Any process of healing is a journey, and it begins from within. Giving yourself an opportunity for recovery helps you gain a better insight into what you need in life. So, when you gain your strength back, you will be ready to manifest it. This could refer to healing your body, mind, or soul. These three elements are parts of an interconnected system, and therefore, each of these aspects affects the other one. A physical illness has an enormous impact on your mental capacity and spirit. Similarly, a wounded soul often affects the functionality of your body and your mind. This chapter contains positive rituals and spells for enhancing one's health and wellness.

It's important to note that while these can restore the balance of the three main aspects of your life, they by no means represent a magical solution for everything. Magick can help you discover where the issue may lie, but its powers lie in your will. Magical solutions can assist you on your healing journey only if you believe they will help restore your spiritual balance. The best way to achieve this is through simple rituals and spells that promote one's well-being. You don't have to burden yourself with complex learning acts of healing magick; what's important is to do what feels best for you.

A Spell to Quiet Your Mind

In this modern world, we are often so preoccupied with everyday tasks that we fail to notice when something inside us goes wrong when it's usually due to this fast-paced, anxiety-ridden life that causes our imbalances. So, before you get to heal yourself, you first have to quieten your mind so you can identify the root of your issues. To do this, you will need to complete a simple ritual. Gather two blue candles, a palo santo stick, a fireproof dish, a piece of white paper, and a blue pen. Light the palo santo stick and the candles, and recite the following affirmation three times:

"*Begone from me, worry and woe!*
I have the strength to break free and the wisdom to know.
As I breathe this sacred smoke, my calm will grow.
I call upon my inner guide to help me take it slow.
My serenity and tranquility will overflow.
With harm to none, blessings to all."

Take deep breaths and let the smoke purify your mind and soul while also passing the pen and the paper over the smoke. When you feel that your mind is sufficiently focused, write down what you feel your intuition is telling you. This is your soul guiding your mind away from stress. Read what you have written a couple of times and contemplate how whatever is on the paper contributes to your spiritual disbalance. More often than not, your worries will be about mundane things without much importance. Try to let it go by redirecting your mind to really important things. Once the anxiety in your mind is replaced with relaxed, positive thoughts, extinguish the palo santo and the candles. Keep the paper with you for at least a couple of days and whenever you feel the stress coming back, reaffirm your priorities. This will help you overcome any stressful situation in the future.

A Self-love Charm

For a white witch, her craft is about embracing nature's powers, and most importantly, her own inner strength. When carrying an emotional burden, you tend to be too critical of yourself, making it difficult to focus on making the world a better place. Fortunately, with a little bit of magick, you can restore your emotional balance and learn to love yourself again. This will enhance your ability to stay connected to others so you can assist on their healing journey as well. To complete a spell that raises confidence, gather five white tealight candles and some flowers in vivid colors. In front of a tall mirror, arrange the flowers in a large circle, and place the candles within it, forming a smaller circle. Sit in the middle of the circles, facing the mirror, and light the candles. Look in the mirror and focus on your best features. Think about what makes you beautiful inside and out, then recite the following spell:

"*I am a beautiful being, regardless of what anyone else says. I can love myself in every way possible.*"

Say the chant four more times, then take a deep breath and embrace your beauty. Leave the candles to burn out. You can do this anytime you have negative thoughts about yourself. Make sure you are alone when doing this so that you can focus entirely on your own issues.

A Spell for Friendship

Having good friends on your side can help you heal any scars much faster. Naturally, we often lose friendships through trying times, which only fills us with more negative energy. However, during these situations, you can also discover new friends. You just have to know where to look for them. Making friends can be hard, but the following spell can help you find people on whom you can rely in good times and *in* bad times. Find a blank postcard, a clear adhesive tape, a gold pen, a bay leaf, and a thin gold ribbon. Take the postcard and write all the characteristics you feel you need in a friend. Attach the bay leaf to the postcard with the adhesive tape and cut off about 12 inches (or 30 cm) of ribbon. Roll up the card, tie it with the ribbon and leave it on your windowsill for about 24 hours. If you do this on a full moon, you can charge your intent with even more powerful natural magick before it's sent out to the universe. When the time is up, take the roll inside your bedroom to keep it close to. Before you know it, the friend who can help you heal the most will enter your life.

Smudging Out Bad Vibes

While it's often applied for replying to dark spells, smudging can be useful for maintaining the positivity a white witch thrives on. You're not just cleaning your home but liberating your mind and purifying your soul as well. That is not to say that you have to mop and vacuum obsessively. In fact, this could disrupt the flow of positive energy, so it's best done in moderation. And most importantly, you have to learn how to do it effectively. Herbs like sage, lavender, and rosemary can all be used for these purposes – besides the cleansing properties, they all have a calming effect on your emotions.

Tie them up a bundle with a cotton string and when you need cleansing, open your windows and doors so the air can circulate through. If you have an AC or fans, turn those on before lighting the end of your smudge bundle. Make sure you blow out the flames, so only the smoke remains, then start walking through your home. Enter each room and circle it in a counter-clockwise motion while reciting your intention – or whatever you need to say at the moment, as long as it's stated in a positive manner. Lastly, you may proceed to smudge your own body as well, alongside whatever item you have in your possession that may evoke bad memories. Similarly, with this ritual, you can get rid of negative energy from your home (and your spirit) by spraying your rooms with a few essential oils mixed with water.

Meditation for Elevating Yourself

One of the easiest ways to get in touch with your emotional needs and address whatever is bothering you is through meditation. It's a simple yet powerful tool that works as the white witch visualizes and affects change. Whether you need healing to move past internal or external obstacles in life, first, you need to gain a clear picture of what those issues are. Meditation techniques rely on breathing regulation, which automatically relieves anxiety and enables you to process pain, whether it is mental or physical. For a white witch, using meditation for healing isn't only about overcoming trauma; it's also a means for reaching goals, which affect many people, not just them.

You can even choose how and when you want to meditate – as long as it gets you to a relaxed state, so you can visualize what it would be like to have everything you want. You can include everything from the way you dress to the way you act in certain situations. Try to conjure a clear picture of various scenarios where you might take advantage of what you have in those pictures. Once you can see what makes you happier, ask yourself what you could do to heal and become able to work towards your goals. By visualizing what you need, instead of what you want, it becomes much easier to identify any emotional issues that are holding you back from becoming a better person and a witch who can truly make a difference.

A Powerful Healing Spell

While this spell may require you to gather a few more ingredients, casting it is actually less complicated than it seems. Moreover, it can provide a very effective solution keeping old or new traumas at bay, so they cannot prevent you from reaching your full potential. For this powerful cleansing spell, you will need three white candles, sandalwood, and mint essential oils, three clear quartz crystals (you may use other colors as well, but white or transparent works best for healing), and three pieces of paper. Make sure you cleanse all these and your space as well before you start casting the spell. Coat the crystals and the candles in the essential oils you have previously mixed. If you are using an altar, put the candles on it by forming a triangular shape. Follow up with a stone in front of each candle. You may use any flat surface in front of you in lieu of an altar if you don't have one set up. Write your target's name (in this case yourself) on each piece of paper and place these between the stones. Focus on raising your energy to heal your emotional trauma and light the three candles.

Repeat the following chant three times:

"Magic mend and candle burn,

Illness leave and health return."

Let the candles burn while visualizing how it would feel to regain your inner harmony for about 30 minutes, then extinguish the candles out with a snuffer. You may repeat this ritual the next night and for as many nights as necessary to help you heal.

A Healing Spell for Unidentified Trauma

Sometimes, despite your best efforts, identifying emotional or spiritual issues becomes challenging. If it's rooted in a very old trauma you weren't even aware of carrying, then even relaxation techniques won't be enough to uncover its true extent. Fortunately, a white witch has a way to heal herself, even without knowing what's blocking her energy. You can do this with the help of six pink candles, an almost dry blue or purple flower, a white one in full blossom, and some soil. Arrange the candles in a semicircle, and light them, starting from the left.

While doing so, cast the following spell:

"Flame of hope and power, restore my strength, hour upon hour.

For they may fill with light like you, and health in me renews.

Drop a petal from the old flower into each candle and say:

Into the fire may the sickness burn away, transform me with each and every day."

Bury the old petals into the soil, and pass the fresh blossom one around the candle while chanting:

"Let smoke rise to the skies while my new health thrives."

Keep meditating while focusing on feeling better and not on why you're feeling bad. This will help flow positive energy into you and cleanse your soul. Let the candles burn as long as you feel necessary for you to ponder on healing, then bury the old petals under the soil. Take apart the blossom and scatter its petals in nature outside of the confinement of your home.

Healing After a Relationship Ends

Whether it's a romantic, a familiar, or a friendship, the ending of a relationship marks a sad moment in our life. During such an emotionally trying time, there is usually a lot of anger involved, and giving into it will not help you to feel better. Instead of that, try casting a healing spell to lift your emotions after ending a relationship with someone. Find a pink and a white candle, sage, and your favorite kind of incense. You will also need healing crystals, preferably pink quartz (symbolizes love) and any other stones of your choice. Cherishing love even after the relationship is over will help you focus on the positive memories to move forward with your life. Use the sage to smudge your space, then put the crystal in front of you (on an altar or any flat surface). Ensure the pink quartz is in the middle and the pink candle next to it. Light this one first and Proceed with lighting the rest of the candles. Repeat the name of the person you need to let go of several times while using the sage again to cleanse yourself. Having done that, light the white candle and recite the following chant:

"I set us free with love.

I'm full of love, so I can let you go with love.

My heart is full and free.

I'm free and at peace."

You may continue this ritual until thinking about the other person doesn't overwhelm you with negative emotions anymore. If necessary, you can even repeat the act as many times as you need to. It may take a long time before you no longer feel sad about the person not being in your life anymore. However, eventually, your heart will become lighter, and your emotional wounds will heal.

A Spell for Banishing Depression

Depression can cause just as much blockage in your magical path as anxiety, so if you feel it's looming over you, it's crucial that you deal with it as soon as possible. The following spell is great for banishing depression, and all you need for it is a yellow and a pink candle. Place the candles in front of you and light them while raising your energy. Close your eyes, and after taking a deep breath, say the following spell:

"Blessed be the love and light

Please come help me this night

My feelings are rather blue

And I don't know what to do.

Help me banish the sadness I feel,

For this feeling has no more appeal
Help me love myself again
So, I feel my heart be light again,
Let me climb up from this hole,
Be with you, mind, body, and soul.
I ask thee on this night please,
Help me to happiness, so mote it be."

While your eyes are still closed, visualize the negative thoughts leaving your mind and getting trapped in the candle flame, which destroys them by burning them. Feel free to continue this ritual for as many days as you need to until there are no more harmful thoughts or emotions left inside of you.

Water Enchantment

Another super easy spell you can try is to charge your water with intent. Despite its simplicity, it's considered one of the most powerful healing spells. It's also a quick spell to cast, which makes it really handy if you want an immediate healing solution. All you need is a glass of water - preferably in a real glass. You may use bottled water, as well, if you only have that at hand, but keep in mind that the plastic may block the flow of natural energy. The water can easily soak up your intention, but this will work better if there is no barrier between it and your mind. Take the glass or bottle between your hands, close your eyes, and focus on your intention. For example, if you have a migraine, try to visualize it being gone. Recite your intent loud and clear, and send as much positive energy into the water as you can. A good way to learn how to channel your energy into an object is by feeling it move through your body. Keep picturing yourself pain-free for two to five minutes, then drink the water within an hour.

Whichever healing spell or ritual you decide to enact will depend on your needs at the moment. The state of your mind, body, and soul will also determine how long your recovery lasts. However, regardless of your progress, you mustn't forget to celebrate small wins. Remember, even tiny progress is better than having no progress at all. Even if you can only get through one day at a time with positive thoughts in your mind, you will be one step closer to fulfilling your purpose as a white witch. Apart from employing magick, you can also help elevate your spirits by doing what you like most. And every time you accomplish something, whether magical or non-magical, your life will be filled with even more positivity.

Chapter 8: Celebrations of the White Witch

When it comes to rituals, some of the most important times of the year during which white witches and Wiccans alike perform positive rituals is during the Sabbats.

However, if you're a beginner to white magic, you may not be familiar with the Sabbats. If this is the case, don't worry. This chapter covers everything you need to know about Sabbats.

It will also provide you with suggestions you can use for your Sabbat ritual celebrations. These are perfect for witches of all experience levels, so regardless of whether you're a newcomer or an experienced practitioner, there's something for everyone.

Understanding the Sabbats

As discussed in previous chapters, white witches and Wiccans are both intrinsically connected to nature and Earth's natural rhythms. These rhythms are celebrated throughout the year, and witches celebrate the Earth's journey around the sun, which is also known as the Wheel of the Year.

However, there are certain days that are more important during the Wheel of the Year than others, and these eight celebrations are known as the Sabbats, and Wiccans and white witches celebrate them as a way of Turning the Wheel.

The Sabbats are divided into the major (greater) and the minor (or lesser) Sabbats.

The minor Sabbats are celebrated on the solstices and equinoxes. The major Sabbats, on the other hand, are celebrated at the midpoint of each set of minor Sabbats.

Let's look at each of the Sabbats, explain their importance, and discuss ritual options you can consider when celebrating them. We'll follow the Wheel of the Year, so you can understand how these days would be celebrated through the year.

Imbolc

This celebration is held on February 2nd and is a celebration of the renewal of life. It marks the end of winter and the beginning of spring - and with it, the beginning of new growth and the first signs of new life.

Imbolc is also popularly known as Candlemas, and as the name implies, it is celebrated as a festival of lights when candles are lit. These candles symbolize the hope of the days growing longer and the sun shining brighter.

Additionally, the word "Imbolc" means "in milk," and milk was traditionally poured on the ground as an offering to the earth. The celebration is one that venerates fertility and the growth of God (following his rebirth on Yule, which we'll discuss later on).

Other names for Imbolc/Candlemas include:
- Groundhog Day
- Feast of the Virgin
- Festival of Milk
- Blessing of the Plow
- Disting

Additionally, this celebration is a time to perform rituals to the goddess Brigid in Celtic Wicca and perform initiations in Dianic Wicca.

As Imbolc rituals often involve candles, it's essential to be mindful of fire safety. Some rituals you can follow include:
- **A Candle Ritual:** Set up your altar, and cast a circle if you wish. Pour sand or salt into a large bowl (or a cauldron). Then, place seven candles of red and white in the sand (or salt), and light

them one after the other. As you do this, call to the fire to purify, heal, and inspire you. You can use a chant you find online or make up one of your own.

- **A Housecleaning Ritual**: Start at your door and go through your home in a clockwise direction, smudging the perimeter of each room. You can use sage, salt, water, and the flame from a blue candle to do so. Use blessing oil to anoint the doors and window sills. If you prefer, you can speak an incantation while doing so. You can also alter this ritual to perform with guests or coven members.

Ostara

Held during the Spring Equinox, this lesser Sabbat is usually celebrated around March 21st. During this Sabbat, the dark and the light are balanced. However, the light is on the rise, and the Wheel of the Year is turning toward the summer.

This Sabbat serves as a celebration of new life and of the world's return to nature. It's a celebration of the fertility of nature. Many people believe it's a good time to begin new things, whether that be relationships, jobs, or anything else.

Other names for the Sabbat include:

- Easter
- Waxing Equinox
- Lady Day
- Alban Eilir

You can celebrate Ostara with the following candle ritual. Remember safety measures, and first set up your altar the way you like it.

You can perform this ritual indoors or outside, depending on your personal preference. You will need three candles – one green, one yellow, and one purple.

First, light the green candle, speaking an incantation acknowledging the new life.

Then, light the yellow candle. Your incantation should acknowledge the importance and life-giving properties of the sun.

Finally, light the purple candle, this time thanking the Goddess and other deities you worship.

Complete the ritual by mixing a little milk and honey and pouring it onto the ground under your altar as an offering to the earth.

Beltane

Celebrated on May 1st, this Sabbat is also known as May Eve. It is often considered to be the most important Sabbat after Samhain.

It is a celebration of fertility and of the approach of summer. It is a time when the crops are growing and is an acknowledgment of human fertility. It is also a popular secular celebration, and traditions include jumping the Bel Fire and dancing around the Maypole. In fact, dancing around the Maypole is a great ritual you can celebrate in your own backyard with your loved ones and coven members!

However, if you're looking for other options, here are some other rituals you can try as well:

- **A Marriage Ritual:** This ritual celebrates the sacred marriage of the Goddess and God. While the ritual is similar to a marriage, it is the Divine Couple getting married instead. Usually, this ritual is celebrated by a coven, with one person chosen to stand in symbolically for the Goddess and one for the God, respectively. The May Queen ties these people together, celebrating the Divine Marriage.

- **A Ritual Celebrating the Sacred Feminine**: To begin, stand with your arms raised to the sky. Speak your thanks to the universe and the Goddess. Then, light a white candle (taking care to follow all fire safety procedures) and place an offering of something important to you on the altar. Now, call upon the Goddess, speaking your thanks and gratitude. Once you have honored the Goddess, you will need to honor the women who have gone before you – place a pebble into a bowl of water for each woman who has impacted your life, speaking out loud each person's name and the impact she has had on you. Finish by honoring your relation to these women and your own strength.

Litha

Held on the Summer Solstice, this Sabbat celebrates the point when summer is at its peak. On this day, the sun shines the longest in the year, and it is also the time when nature is at its peak and at its strongest.

This Sabbat is a day of giving thanks to the sun being at its peak. Heat that is too strong can damage crops, and the change of seasons allows them to continue growing without major issues. At the same time, Wiccans mark Litha with a recognition of both the fertility and the impending death of God on Samhain.

Other names for the Sabbat include:

- Midsummer / Midsummer's Eve
- Whitsuntide
- Vestalia

Here are a few rituals you can celebrate Litha with:

- **Tool Recharging Ritual**: With the sun's power at its peak, you can take advantage of recharging your magic tools. First, clean them with sea salt or by leaving them in the sunlight for at least an hour. Once your tools are clean, focus on your purpose or goal (if you have one) or simply a desire to recharge your tools and place them outside, under the full light of the sun. You can also speak words of intention over them to concentrate the energy of the sun – these words are dependent on your goals and personal to each practitioner.

- **Backyard Barbeque Ritual**: This is a great way to celebrate Litha with your loved ones. Decorate your backyard with symbols of the season, and cast a circle with the help of your guests. Invoke the elements in festive, unique ways, such as waving sparklers as a way to invoke fire or squirting water with squirt guns when calling on water. Prepare your food, and start your ceremony when the food is ready. Place a platter of food on your altar and form a circle in front of the altar. Speak words honoring the sun and the spirits of the land, and thank the earth for your food. Then, invite each guest to your altar to make an offering. Once all guests have done this, complete the ceremony by blessing the food you placed on the altar and then dig into your meal!

Lammas

Held on August 1st, this is a celebration of the first harvest of the year and of the approach of fall. At the same time, it's a reminder of the coming winter and is marked by the first signs of the cold.

Other names for Lammas include:
- Lughnasadh
- First Harvest
- Cerealia

Lammas is both a day of celebration and of solemnity – it is a reminder of the quickly approaching death of the god being celebrated. Honoring this sacrifice is one of the key rituals you can perform on Lammas.

This ritual is meant for a coven, and you will need a loaf of bread with the figure of the god baked into it. Additionally, you should light a small fire in a brazier, taking care to follow fire safety regulations.

The High Priestess will start the ritual with an incantation. Then, each member of the coven will make a doll out of straw representing themselves, energizing with their individual essence. Again, the High Priestess will speak an incantation.

After this, you and your coven should circle your altar three times, going faster each time to raise energy. One at a time, each person present should cast their doll into the fire and speak of their sacrifice for the year.

Once this is done, your coven should share the loaf of bread among yourself and complete it by sharing a cup of wine (or water).

Mabon

This Sabbat is a celebration of the Autumnal Equinox and is held around September 21st. Like Ostara, it is a point when the light and the dark are in perfect balance and night and day are of equal length – but this time, darkness is on the rise.

Mabon marks the second harvest of the year and serves as the conclusion of the harvest season. The year and the cycle of life are drawing closer, and God is preparing for his impending death.

Other names for Mabon include:
- Wine Harvest
- Alban Elfer
- Harvest

Mabon is a time to celebrate the triple goddess's crone aspect, as well as the archetype of the Dark Mother and the parts of the Goddess that may not always be comforting but should still be acknowledged.

Additionally, many practitioners use Mabon to hold rituals devoted to Demeter and Persephone, as it was Persephone's abduction and Demeter's response that birthed the first winter.

Here's a ritual to Demeter and Persephone you can hold on Mabon.

First, decorate your altar with symbols of the two goddesses. You will need two candles for this ritual – one in harvest colors for Demeter and one in black for Persephone. Make sure you take appropriate fire safety steps.

Light the black candle first while facing the altar, speaking an incantation that acknowledges the upcoming winter, Persephone's descent into the Underworld, and Demeter's grief.

Then, light the candle for Demeter, reciting an incantation that acknowledges and honors Demeter's grief over her kidnapped daughter.

Next, open a pomegranate. Remove six seeds and place them on the altar. Recite an incantation acknowledging the upcoming winter, the cycle of life, and honoring and celebrating the Dark Mother and the crone.

Finally, take a sip of ceremonial wine (or grape juice), and place the chalice on your altar. Then, call out to the goddesses who represent the darker parts of human nature, embracing these aspects in your own life and thanking them.

Samhain

Celebrated on October 31st, this is perhaps the most important of all the Sabbats. It symbolizes the end of the year and the cycle of life, and it is the time when the veil between the worlds is the thinnest it has been all year long.

Samhain marks the death of God and is a day of remembrance for the dead. It is a time of honoring those that have gone before and preparing for the "death" of nature – winter.

It is often regarded as a good time to communicate with the dead and is also considered to be an auspicious night for divination.

There are numerous ways to celebrate Samhain, each of them extremely personal to the practitioner. However, here's a ritual honoring the ancestors you can try.

First, decorate your altar with pictures of your family, heirlooms, and other important items representing your loved ones. You should especially add things important to the ancestors – a grave rubbing, if possible, a family tree, a postcard from any loved ones who have passed, flags which symbolize countries they lived in. A cluttered altar is okay for this ritual.

Host a meal near the altar. This can be a meal for yourself, or for all your family. Your dinner table should have space for each family member who has gone before and who you are honoring. There should also be extra space and a plate for your ancestors as a whole. Your meal table should include plenty of apples, dark bread, fall vegetables, and wine (or cider).

Before the meal, light a candle on your altar for each relative who has passed during the year, and then for other loved ones, saying each person's name aloud as you light their candle. If this is a ritual you're hosting with the rest of your family, the oldest adult should lead the ceremony. Alternatively, you can host it as a solo ritual as well.

Speak an incantation acknowledging and honoring the ancestors and your loved ones who have passed. Serve everyone at your table a generous helping of each dish, remembering to serve a helping on the ancestors' plate first. As you eat, share memories of your loved ones with family members.

After your meal, share a glass of wine (or cider). Each person should take a sip from the glass and recite their genealogy. When the cup has made its way around the table, place it in front of the altar. The youngest person should close the ritual with an incantation of remembrance.

Yule

Held on the Winter Solstice, Yule celebrates the rebirth of God and the upcoming New Year. It is a festival of renewal and rebirth. Though it is the longest night of the year, it is also an acknowledgment that the days will only get longer (and brighter) from here.

Yule celebrations often incorporate more secular Christmas traditions, especially if you're celebrating with non-practitioner friends and family. Many celebrations (like gift-giving and bringing springs and wreaths of evergreens like holly and mistletoe into your home) are the same for both Yule and Christmas.

If you're looking to host a Yule ritual, you can host one that everyone can enjoy, including your non-practitioner family.

For this ritual, you'll first need to make a Yule log. This will be made of a log, pine cones, dried berries, cuttings of evergreens, feathers, sticks of cinnamon, and cloth (or paper) ribbon.

Wrap the log loosely with the ribbon, inserting your branches, feathers, and cuttings underneath. Glue on the pinecones, berries, and cinnamon sticks to complete your Yule log.

On Yule, host a meal and have the log as the centerpiece decoration of the table. After the meal, put the log into the fire, and as the log burns, all practitioners should form a circle around it, moving clockwise around it and welcoming back the sun. Everyone at the celebration (practitioners and non-practitioners alike) can then take a moment to share something they are thankful for that relates to family.

Once everyone has shared, move clockwise around the log and fire once more to end the ritual. Save some of the Yule logs to add to next year's Yule fire.

Chapter 9: Spellcrafting for Good Purposes

Spellcrafting is the act of using occult powers to practice magic and cast spells. White magic is all about using these powers for good causes. It's about channeling the good energy within each one of us and using it to bring peace. That said, all spells used in white magic are for good purposes. This is why you can't practice white magic if your soul is not in the right place. Many spells can be used to help others and spread peace instead of just healing yourself. It takes selfless intentions and unshakeable ethics to practice these spells and use them for the greater good. In this chapter, we teach you the basics of getting into spell crafting and how to use it for selfless manifestations.

Spellwork

According to multiple ancient beliefs, there is an established flowing life force existing in every living organism. This force has been given many names depending on the culture; for example, it is referred to as Qi in traditional Chinese medicine, Ka in the ancient Egyptian religions, and Prana in Hindu philosophy. All these names only attempt to describe a force or essence that represents existence. This powerful essence is known to animate everything natural around us.

Many divination practices believe that a reflection of the entire cosmology exists within each living organism. According to this belief, all microcosms embody all macrocosms. Inherently, spell-making is the art of identifying and directing the energy within for the purpose of making supernatural changes. This process doesn't include the use of any external tools such as rules, books, or any special privileges. In fact, all you need is your magical intention. It is said that spells are practically anything that you do with magical intentions, except for incantations. They are spells that are created using words rather than intentions.

The only difference between the normal things you do on a daily basis, and magical or occult practices, is your connection to the actions you take or the intentions you have. In other words, you make your actions magical with your intentions, and you choose whether you want them to be magical or not. So basically, rituals and objects are never magical; they just help us channel our innate magical energies.

The Main Principles for Spellcrafting

The most successful spells are cast with purpose. You need a burning desire or need before you can attempt to practice white magic rituals. This is why your intentions matter the most; you can try to cast a spell as a response to a certain emotion you have, for example, wanting to exploit a business opportunity or the need to know more about casting spells as part of your growing interest. However, it's not recommended to cast spells when you're experiencing extreme emotional distress. Spells are all about reflecting your manifestations and are strongly affected by your temperament during the creation of the spell. So, you need a clear mind when casting spells; it's important that your thoughts and feelings are in the right place so you can be direct and honest with your energy. If you feed your spells with bad energy, you may not like the erratic outcomes, so make sure you set your intentions at the beginning. Use your wisdom, focus, and empathy to direct good-natured energy in your practices.

There are unlimited ways you can cast a spell. However, there are different types of spells depending on the concept behind each. These concepts are controlled by the main attributes for casting spells, and here are some of these attributes:

Correspondence

Correspondences are the connections between tangible and intangible things. The tangible things are the tools you use to create or craft your spells. These tools can also be the time or place you choose to cast your spells. For example, you can use the correspondence of planets to cast a love spell. Although love spells are not really considered good-natured or for good purposes. However, Mercury, for instance, represents communication, while Mars represents determination. Venus is the planet that represents romance; these planets may also symbolize the days of the week. You can use these celestial bodies as tools in your spells. For example, cast your love spell on a Friday, which is the day that represents Venus, the planet of romance. It will help make your spell more effective.

These correspondences were used for centuries to create connections between intangibles and physical items. However, many modern correspondences were also established, such as mirrors which were believed to act as vessels for incantation. This can be seen in the example of saying "Bloody Mary" three times in the mirror. Much research can be found in this area, so make sure to find the connections that catch your interest and use them in your spells.

The Concept of Antipathy and Sympathy

To practice magic with more experience in the science of energies and how they flow, you have to understand that the phenomenon where two things attract one another is known as sympathy. On the other hand, when two things repel one another, the phenomenon is called antipathy. Sympathy suggests that if two objects or entities are tied or attracted in one realm, they are bound to stay connected in any other realm. Sympathy is commonly used in love spells, such as the practice of slowly moving two symbolic candles closer to each other; when the candles touch, it is believed that a union is formed. In this spell, the two symbolic candles are bound together using a honeysuckle vine to create a sweet connection.

Sympathy is also used in another love spell where you carve on a seven-day red candle the name and astrological sign or birthday of the person you want to cast a spell on. Before lighting the candle, you genuinely and openly set your intentions then you let the candle burn until the end. Sometimes, it may not be safe to keep the candle lit for too long. You can simply snuff it out and repeat your intentions before lighting it up again. Just know that when the candle is completely burnt, your spell will be completed. You may need to observe the flame of the candle when it's lit. Does the flame dim very often? Is it strong? Is it moving erratically? These indications should help you find out how your desired romance will unfold.

On the other hand, antipathy is the repelling of forces. Antipathy can be seen in many bad-natured spells but also in good-intended spells as part of self-care. For example, you may need to push someone outside of your life because of how toxic they are to you. In this case, you can tie a candle tightly with wire or twine and place it in the freezer with the intention to keep this person outside of your life. This refers to the saying of "Put them on ice." Another antipathic spell to permanently remove people from your life is done by writing their name in a letter and mailing the letter to an undeliverable location. Just make sure you don't put your return address on the letter so that the spell works perfectly. It's all about the symbolism and the intentional aspects of your spell.

Contagion

To understand the dynamics and basics of good-purpose spells, you have to grasp the concept of contagion and how it works when it comes to white magic. The idea of contagion spells was built on the concept that once two things are in contact, they are always in contact. Likewise, when you send your charm over to someone you love by sending them something that is yours, you manage to send your notion and stay in contact with them as long as they possess this one item or object. This notion believes that once two entities are in contact in any particular way, they will remain in contact even if they were physically separated somehow.

To participate in contagious magic, you have to lay your hands on something that belongs to the person or entity you target with your spell. This thing can be a lock of their hair, a napkin that they used, or even a piece of their clothing to represent their essence. It just needs to be an object that already has a cosmic connection to the entity or individual you're targeting. If the connection is established, you'll succeed in amplifying your magical intentions through contagion.

Repetition

Repetition helps you strengthen and build stronger connections through your magic practices. Repetition helps you create a rhythm that increases your intention and focus during the spell casting process. Not only that, but it also brings a cyclical aspect that adds a powerful heat to your incantations and gives them a deeper energetic charge. When you repeatedly engage in a magical correspondence such as writing your crush's name on a piece of paper, sweeping the house with the intention of clearing out negative energy or even reciting a chant, you purposely create a spell-based habit that helps you deepen your enchanted bonds, and ensure an unbreakable bond between the magical and the physical.

People will often opt for rhymes to promote repetition in their spells. Rhymes work very well with the human brain as they leave a psychological impression and become easier to remember over time.

Getting Started with Spellcrafting

The only tools you need when crafting magical spells are your intentions and beliefs. However, the beginning can seem a little intimidating for beginners. This chapter will help you get around the dynamics of this practice and master it like a true professional spell crafter. With that in mind, you can charge any object with your energy if you have the right intentions. The best thing is you don't even need to purchase expensive healing crystals to perform your incantations and perfect your spells. You can simply use black pepper, cinnamon, sugar, or cayenne pepper to add to your chosen oils and create magical infusions or spell recipes. These spices are very powerful when it comes to manifestation and contagion magic. Practitioners also use cooking pots as cauldrons to prepare their potions, while almost any candle can be used as a connected magical device. To truly practice white magic, you have to learn how to charge objects with energy and use tangible tools for connecting with the intangible.

You also need to understand that once you deem any object as enchanted, it remains that way. You can use objects for double purposes. For example, you can use wine glasses to prepare different magical potions, but you can't then use them to entertain your guests and serve wine in them at the same time unless your spell involves serving wine to your guests in those glasses. The tools you use for your magical endeavors maintain the energy you charge them with, so make sure you keep track of the mystical devices you leave around.

Another concept to wrap your mind around when practicing white magic is the location in which you choose to cast your spell or ritual. Physical thresholds such as windows and doorways may act as cosmic entrances and portals to other realms or different worlds. Even the smallest cracks in the floorboards may symbolize openings and spaces between different dimensions. These spaces are actually good for practicing white magic or casting good-natured spells. It may also be more helpful to cast your spell during the intersection between day and night or in the period of seasonal equinoxes. This is when the sun makes its way across the celestial equator or when the length of the day is equal to the length of night.

The location you choose can symbolize many things relating to your spell. However, be sure to close any door you open during the ritual to symbolize completing or finishing your spell. You can either create a ritual for closing your spell or simply say "goodbye" to the place you used for casting your spell.

Good Intentions

The one rule to practicing white magic or casting good-purposed spells is to have good intentions and avoid any malicious urges or energies which may hurt you or other people. The karmic principle of magic states that energies comply with a threefold return law. This means any energy you direct will be redirected back at you with three times its real power. You have to be very careful with the energies you let out because everything returns. If you're not really sure about a certain spell, or you're just confused about your feelings, don't cast that spell. Your intentions matter the most when practicing white magic, so if they're not in the right frame of mind, you won't like the outcome. Make sure the only fuel to your curiosity is more kindness and love.

Instructions for Casting a Spell for Good Purposes

At this point, you may be wondering how it works in real life and what the steps to cast a real good-natured spell are. This is the part where we tell you how to apply the above teachings and craft your own magical spell. To cast a spell, you have to be internally ready to send off positive energy and trust in the process. Spells don't work immediately, and many would lose their patience waiting for their spells to show results. You have to entirely believe that your spell will work for your intentions to align with the process. Magic is all about believing and willpower to use this endless power for good purposes.

You'll need to get started by defining your goals or the purpose behind your magical spell. What is it that you want to achieve? With all the positive energy in you, you may want to use spells to help a loved one get through their dark times. This is considered a good purpose, and if you have the right determination, you'll be able to connect with their energy and guide them to the right path. You'll need physical tools to perform the spell, and you'll need to establish clear intentions.

So, in this example, you'll need to focus all your energy on sympathy, and you'll need to be willing to send your positive energy to the person you think is struggling. This can be symbolized by the simplest gestures of sympathy, such as sending them a bouquet of flowers to show them how much you care. Before sending the flowers, you may need to hold the flowers tightly as you practice a magical incantation wishing them the best of luck or simply to end their grief. Focus on being willing to support them with your energy so that the flowers can carry your contagious positive energy and transmit it to them.

The flowers will embody your energy and spread it through this person's place as they keep watering them. When the flowers finally die, this will represent the completion of your spell, and you'll have effectively transmitted the mystical positive energy to them.

Other people use these good-natured spells for abundance and healing. If you're responsible for looking after your family and you cast a spell for financial abundance, it's considered a spell for good purpose because it helps you support those around you. These rituals are similar to tossing a coin in the well and wishing for good luck or financial prosperity. It's all about believing in the energy you exude and how it's going to be returned to you if you set the right intentions. So, you can practice the same concepts and toss a coin inside of a well with the intention that you wish for financial abundance in your life. Make sure you spend enough time with the coin to reflect on your wishes and resonate or vibrate on the same frequency as your goals. By believing in the process, your wishes will be multiplied, and you'll receive your positive energy back.

Meditation for Good-Natured Spells

Meditation serves as a powerful tool when it comes to practicing magic and focusing on your spiritual side. Not only does it improve our brain function and help us take care of ourselves, but it also centers our energies and makes it easier for us to read our thoughts and intentions. Meditation is a core tool for manifestation. You just have to think of the energy you want to manifest, and meditation will work its magic. During a meditation session, you observe your thoughts and filter them out to identify your core desires. You can also use it for many other mental purposes, such as relieving stress and grounding your thoughts when you're feeling overwhelmed.

When casting a selfless spell, it's important that you face your thoughts and determine what you really want from the outcome of the spell. Is it really a good purpose? Is it really for the benefit of others? You can easily answer these questions once you sit comfortably in a quiet place and reflect on your inner voices. It's so easy to align with your inner self when you're meditating and observing your thoughts. This is why meditation is an essential practice for anyone practicing white magic. It's because the only way to channel selfless energy is through taking the time to manifest this energy and direct it in the right direction.

Casting a good-natured spell is as easy as wishing for good luck. Anyone can cast a spell for a good purpose at home. All you need is your magical intentions and some knowledge of how spells work and the methods which make them come true. Spells usually depend on the mentality of the person casting them. It takes a true believer to make a spell work. This is why you shouldn't be practicing white magic spells if you're not really into the idea or you're having second thoughts about it.

Chapter 10: Working with Spirit Guides

In Wiccan culture, white magic has always solicited the assistance of magical forces to ensure certain spells work successfully. A person practicing white magic can have either one or multiple spirit guides to help them navigate through complex spells and rituals. As a white witch, you don't always have to work alone and can rely on the spiritual guidance of certain mythical creatures to help you through your journey. These guides work in mysterious ways, and their positive effects on your life and your spells can be observed in many forms. For instance, good spiritual guidance from the correct source can bring you closer to better opportunities or simply accelerate the effects of your spellwork.

To communicate with your spirit guides, you must first understand what they are and how they function. Only then will you be able to connect and interact with them successfully. Continue reading to learn how spirit guides work, how to recognize your own personal spirit guides, and how to communicate with them effectively.

Types of Spirit Guides and How They Work

Depending on the personality traits of an individual, spirit guides are assigned, and these can help guide you through specific spellwork and make positive affirmations more powerful. These spirit guides come in many forms, some visible, while some are just mystic creatures guiding us through our spiritual journey. What these guides have in common is that their positive energies can be manifested through a series of spells and rituals to connect you with them. However, before you can connect with your specific guides, you must first learn everything there is to know about them. Here's how spirit guides work and what forms they can exist in.

1. Archangels

Archangels are the most powerful angels, with stronger powers and a substantially higher energy signature than the other angels. Your work will be considerably impacted if you choose an archangel to be your spirit guide, whether for a specific spell ritual or for your overall white magic affirmations, due to the high energy shift they bring. Each archangel has a unique attribute, and depending on the spell, a different archangel can be called each time to serve as your spirit guide. For instance, if you're working on a healing spell, whether emotional or physical, the archangel Raphael would be the most suitable spirit guide to bring power to your spell since he's connected to healing.

2. Guardian Angels

Guardian angels, unlike archangels, are individually tailored for every person. Each of us has a personal guardian angel who is in charge of our happiness and well-being. Guardian angels are the most devoted to you and your affirmations out of all the spirit guides. You can think of them as divine life coaches who will guide you through any challenging times in your life. Simply acknowledging the presence of your guardian angel(s) during your spellwork or affirmation routine will help you connect with them. They will be able to make your white magic journey a bit easier.

3. Departed Loved Ones

Spirit guides come in many forms, and even your close loved ones who have passed away can act as guides through various journeys in your life. Compared to other types of spirit guides, your deceased loved ones can only act as your spirit guides through a process only if they choose it. You can't manifest their guidance and positive energy without their consent or specifically choose which guide you want. It's worth noting that a human spirit guide might be any human soul who wishes to assist you. They don't have to be related to you or even know you personally.

4. Spirit Animals

Spirit animals are the most common form of spirit guides that help you in your magical journey. Not only do they provide specific positive energy for your spells, but they also act as a crutch through difficult times and when you are casting intricate spells. A person can have just one or multiple spirit animals guiding them. Every spirit animal has a trait that helps you navigate through different stages of life. Here's a list of spirit animals that you might have and their specific attributes associated with spells and overall life.

- **Bear** - One of the most powerful spirit animals, bears, are associated with the outdoors and connected to earth and nature. Consequently, they can help assist in earth binding spells and similar
- **Cat** - The cat spiritual animal is attributed with curiosity and adventure. It also helps give you a sense of patience through the adversities of life.
- **Butterfly** - The butterfly is associated with transformation and change and can help ease difficult transitions in life.
- **Dove** - The dove is considered to be a hopeful and optimistic spirit animal. It is associated with blessings and peace and helps with new beginnings.
- **Dolphin** - Dolphin spirit guides serve as communicators and unifiers. They represent wisdom and help fix broken connections.
- **Deer** - A deer is associated with confidence and success. It is a highly intuitive spirit animal that helps to guide you in every aspect of life. If you're uncertain about a spell or ritual, a deer spirit animal will help you get more confident in your abilities and ease your process.
- **Fox** - Associated with the art of camouflage, it helps you grow with your surroundings and can help you with spells concerning toxic detachments.
- **Elephant** - The elephant spirit animal symbolizes spiritual understanding, wisdom, and gentleness.
- **Frog** - The frog spirit animal helps you with healing spells for both physical and emotional wounds. It helps to heal past traumas and live in the present.
- **Hawk** - Considered to be extremely compassionate and empathetic, the hawk spirit guide helps you view things from different perspectives.

- **Horse** – Horse spirit guides can help you become extremely goal-oriented and help you focus on what really matters. You'll observe a significant increase in your productivity spells' effectiveness through this guide.
- **Mouse** – The mouse represents the importance of attention to detail and how you shouldn't ignore the smaller things in life. It makes you appreciative of little things.
- **Lion** – The lion symbolizes courage and authority. It can help with spells to boost your leadership skills.
- **Peacock** – Peacock guides represent the importance of reinvention. It helps you understand that it's never too late to change.
- **Owl** – The owl spirit guide helps you see things that would otherwise be invisible and helps you with spells to understand the deeper meaning of life.
- **Tiger** – The tiger spirit animal, considered one of the most intuitive spirit guides. It helps you choose the best possible path for yourself.
- **Turtle** – A turtle spirit animal helps you become wiser and at peace. It can help boost spells related to spiritual growth and development.
- **Wolf** – The wolf guide tends to follow primal instincts above all and hence helps connect to the intelligent and instinctive part of your personality.

5. Ascended Masters

Buddha, Gandhi, Mother Mary, and many other great and inspirational figures are examples of ascended masters. These folks led extraordinary lives and now serve as role models and spirit guides to help us navigate the trials and tribulations of life. No matter what faith or culture you follow, these spirit guides will support you through your positive spells and affirmations. People are usually linked to these gurus through their ideals and beliefs.

6. The Universe

The essence of our universe is one of the most powerful spirit guides, continuously giving us signs and directions to help us. You can conceive of it as a complex web of energy that binds all living things together. The universe is able to detect even the tiniest changes in your life and steers you in the direction of what is best for you. Furthermore, external circumstances and astrological events have a tremendous impact on the power of your spells. You'll be able to get the most out of your rituals and practices if you allow the universe to guide you and your affirmations.

How to Find Your Spirit Guide

Our spirit guides are meant to be everywhere around us, just waiting for us to find them. Every day, we receive innumerable signs and indications from our guides, and it is our responsibility to identify them. You can use these steps to better identify and interpret the messages provided by spirit guides.

1. Ask for More Signs

Humans were given free will, and through it, we're supposed to ask for more signs and indications to help us find our spiritual guides. In essence, think of yourself as a powerful spiritual being, and with all your energy manifesting your request either written in a journal or a strong thought during meditation exercises. It's possible that you might be getting signs but not looking closely enough to see them.

2. Learn about Universe Signs

It's important to understand how your spirit guides give you signs. To do this, you should familiarize yourself with the language of the universe. There are some common ways the universe communicates with people, which include a frequent appearance of spirit animals, meaningful numbers, wise words from someone, the four psychic clairs, music, and through prophetic dreams. The more you know about these signs, the better you'll be at identifying them and finding your spirit guide.

3. Acknowledge Them

After you learn how to recognize the signs, it's time for you to start acknowledging them. You can do this through mindful meditation, mentioning these signs in your journal, or discussing them with a close friend. When the universe observes that you are more open to guidance, it will send you more guidance and clearer signs.

4. Interpret the Signs

It's great that you're beginning to recognize the various signs delivered to you on a daily basis, but what precisely do they mean? To grasp what your received indications mean, you must think about each one for some time and try to interpret, evaluate, and search for a deeper meaning in them. You can use oracle cards to best forecast the clear meaning of a universe sign for this.

5. Act On the Signs

The signs you receive from your spiritual guides are supposed to make your journey easier, but they will only be effective if you actually act on these signs. Plus, when we take action on these signs, the guidance we always get increases. When we take just a single step towards our dreams, they take ten steps towards us. This is why it's important to actually work towards your goals.

How to Connect and Communicate with Your Spirit Guide

As you are aware, spirit guides enter your life by sending you signs, which are also known as synchronicities. These are profound coincidences that leave you thinking about a deeper significance, prompting you to act on these signs. For example, if you've just had a disagreement with your partner and come across an article or book about repairing relationships, this is a meaningful coincidence or could be a direct message from your spirit guide. Similarly, these guides offer signs and assist in the navigation of white magic spell work. For millennia, Wiccan white magic traditions have relied on spirit guides to help them with spell casting. However, to fully harness the support of your spirit guides, you must first learn how to connect and communicate with them, which you can do by following these simple instructions.

1. Start a Spirit Guide Journal

To improve communication between you and your spiritual guides, the next best thing to understanding their signs is to create a journal devoted to your spiritual journey. Although your spirit guides know you well, it can be pretty powerful to write down your requests and ask them for assistance. Just the act of writing down what you require from them will significantly increase their guidance.

What you can do is write a weekly letter to your guides expressing gratitude for anything you feel like they've helped with recently. Next, write down your requests or ask for assistance with specific problems you're facing or spells you need to cast.

2. Get to Know Your Guides

A great idea to get closer to your spirit guides is to give them a name. This makes them more real and helps you acknowledge their presence and help. Whether your guide is a guardian angel or a spirit animal, naming them will help you get closer to them over a period of time.

What you can do is name your spirit guide intuitively or see if their name comes up in one of the signs or synchronicities they send. Names could be based on personalities, and through their guidance, you will feel the difference between every guide's personality. Some might be serious and motivated, while others can be playful and laid back.

3. Surrender Your Issues to Your Guides

When you're stuck and severely frustrated by a problem, it can be difficult to read the signs, and you end up hitting a blank wall. In these cases, you should completely surrender your issue to your guides, even if just to give yourself a break. This will allow your brain to relax, and fresh new insights will come pouring in. It will also give your spirit guides the chance to tilt things in your favor.

What you can do is practice releasing an issue completely, even just temporarily. Try to let go of all the worry, and meditate. Clear your mind, and remove all strategies and worrying.

4. Learn More about Them

When you research more about spirit guides, you'll find so much information to help you connect with them. Look for experts who can help you on this subject and ensure you get empowering guidance.

What you can do: attend a workshop, read an article, or take an online class about spirit guides and how to understand them better. There are many resources that will help you interpret their signs better and hence promote effective communication.

5. Develop Regular Spiritual Practices

If you want to create a better connection with your spirit guides, it's a good idea to develop regular spiritual practices which will strengthen your relationship. For example, you can carry out an oracle card reading every morning, mindful practice meditation, or attend a class with other spiritual people.

What you can do is create regular spiritual practices in your life and carry out a spiritual ritual in the next few weeks. This can include a new moon ritual, an affirmation spell, or anything else to help create a routine.

6. Improve Your Intuition

Every one of us has intuition, which can be developed by studying and understanding the four main intuitive pathways. These include clairaudience, where you hear guiding voices in your head; clairvoyance, where you see guidance in the form of images; claircognizance, where you get breakthroughs in your mind and, finally; clairsentience, where you feel guidance in the form of a shift in energy, and emotions.

What you can do is practice your intuition skills on something that doesn't hold too much risk. Test your hunches through your intuitive abilities to get a greater sense of this ability.

7. Communicate Via Thoughts

This may seem like useless advice, but communicating via your thoughts to ask for assistance from your spirit guides is one of the best ways to communicate with them.

What you can do is ask for assistance with something you're currently struggling with. Remember to also get support elsewhere, like from a friend or loved one.

8. Use a Divination Tool

Wiccan magic has been using divination tools to communicate with spirit guides, as they are considered the most effective and convenient way to communicate. There are many types of divination tools you can use, which include tarot cards, oracle cards, and many other things. Make sure you choose the most suitable tool for your spells.

Wiccan magic techniques have used positive white magic for millennia and are still in use today. Your spirit guides can include angels, humans, and animals, even the universe; each and every guide exists to ensure that you pass your challenges with ease. There are many spells in white magic that require the guidance of specific spirit guides to ensure completion. Guides also ensure maximum effectiveness of the spell that is cast. In short, make sure that you have a good relationship with your guides and that you understand how to identify and interpret their signs.

Conclusion

While Wicca in itself is a fairly new religion, the use of white magic dates back centuries. Through the years, this elemental practice of following the energy of nature has been found in many cultures. However, since it relies on subtle interactions with natural elements and selfless use of one's own powers, white magic was often shadowed by its black counterpart. Since, for many, the modern world has made it very challenging to thrive, more and more people are turning to nature for spiritual guidance and self-growth. If you are one of them, hopefully, you found this book helpful enough for the beginning of your Wiccan journey. In it, you were given all the tools required to fill your life with true happiness. From the magic spells designed to help you spread the light and peace amongst your circle to the rituals you may use to obtain your own safety and harmony – now you have it all.

From here on, it will be up to you to learn the ins and outs of spellcasting and practice the techniques until you master them to perfection. If you are a beginner, this may take some time to accomplish, but don't be discouraged if you are not able to help someone right away. Feel free to use breathing techniques like meditation to help you remain focused on the task at hand. Remember your goal is to protect those in need through the beneficial spells of white magic, and the blessing will come back to you. Never use the craft for destruction or harm, as the negative energy can find its way back to you. You shouldn't use magic on someone without their knowledge either because doing so will constitute a malicious act. Even if you are casting a protection spell thinking it will benefit the recipient – if you do this without their consent, this goes against the main principle of white magic. There are very few rules to the Craft of Wiccan white magic, but following these is crucial for a successful practice.

While the rituals and spells of white magic are designed to bring happiness to others, ultimately, the one who will benefit from your own Craft will be you. All the blessings you cast upon others will fill you with so much positivity that it becomes much easier for you to manifest your own desires. This action is paramount for effectively resolving many aspects of your life. Don't be surprised if the blessings you receive back don't come in the way you may expect them to do. White magic spells promote casting away all the negativity from your life, which causes healing in a way you really need it. They help provide harmony, peace, and protection not just from malicious magic but from your own emotional scars as well. Our success is often limited by emotional baggage we carry from the past without even being aware of it - but it doesn't have to be that way. So go on, and prepare yourself to cast the circle that will change your life and, at the same time, make the world a better place as well.

Here's another book by Mari Silva that you might like

Your Free Gift
(only available for a limited time)

Thanks for getting this book! If you want to learn more about various spirituality topics, then join Mari Silva's community and get a free guided meditation MP3 for awakening your third eye. This guided meditation mp3 is designed to open and strengthen ones third eye so you can experience a higher state of consciousness. Simply visit the link below the image to get started.

https://spiritualityspot.com/meditation

Or, Scan the QR code!

Resources

2spirts. (2022, October 8). *Protection spells*. 2spirits.com. https://www.2spirits.com/protection-spell

Basics of magic: Clearing and charging ritual tools -. (2017, June 16). Wicca Living. https://wiccaliving.com/clearing-charging-ritual-tools/

Beginner's guide to spell candle magick and colour correspondences. (n.d.). ForestofWisdom. Retrieved from https://forestofwisdom.com.au/blogs/into-the-forest/beginner-s-guide-to-spell-candle-magick-and-colour-correspondences

Beyer, C. (2011, May 8). *The five element symbols of fire, water, air, earth, spirit*. Learn Religions. https://www.learnreligions.com/elemental-symbols-4122788

Kelmenson, K. (2021, October 11). *The spiritual meaning of moon phases*. Spirituality & Health. https://www.spiritualityhealth.com/the-spiritual-meaning-of-moon-phases

Mabon house. (n.d.). Mabon House. Retrieved from https://www.mabonhouse.co/mabon

Magical properties of colors. (2017, June 23). Wicca Living. https://wiccaliving.com/magical-properties-colors/

Murphy-Hiscock, A. (2020). *Spellcrafting: Strengthen the power of your craft by creating and casting your own unique spells*. Simon & Schuster Audio.

Plants and herbs used for magic. (n.d.). Bluerelicsflowers.com. Retrieved from https://www.bluerelicsflowers.com/Plants-and-Herbs-Used-for-Magic

Samhain (samain) - the Celtic roots of Halloween. (n.d.). Newgrange.com. Retrieved from https://www.newgrange.com/samhain.htm

Shade, P. (n.d.). *The supernatural side of plants – CornellBotanicGardens*. Cornellbotanicgardens.org. Retrieved from https://cornellbotanicgardens.org/the-supernatural-side-of-plants/

Stardust, L. (2021, March 1). *How to use the moon's eight phases to live your best life*. Oprah Daily. https://www.oprahdaily.com/life/a35684513/moon-phases-manifest-meaning-astrology/

Ward, K. (2021, December 23). *Your everything-you-need-to-know intro to candle magick*. Cosmopolitan. https://www.cosmopolitan.com/lifestyle/a31133533/candle-magic-colors-meaning/

(N.d.-a). Mit.edu. Retrieved from https://web.mit.edu/pipa/www/rede.html

(N.d.-b). Theembroideredforest.com. Retrieved from https://theembroideredforest.com/blogs/wicca/how-to-cast-a-circle

British Library. (n.d.). Www.Bl.Uk. Retrieved from https://www.bl.uk/shakespeare/articles/prospero-a-renaissance-magus

Middle Eastern religion – Middle Eastern worldviews and basic religious thought. (n.d.). In

Encyclopedia Britannica.

White vs. Black magic in the renaissance. (n.d.). Cedarcrest.Edu. Retrieved from http://www2.cedarcrest.edu/academic/eng/lfletcher/tempest/papers/DSpina.htm

JustCode. (n.d.). Wiccan basics – meditation – general pagan – the white goddess. Retrieved Thewhitegoddess.co.uk website:

http://www.thewhitegoddess.co.uk/articles/general_pagan/wiccan_basics_-_meditation.asp

Mueller, M., Kovnesky, L., & Snyder, M. (2020, October 26). Hold my broom: Here's real talk

from a "real" witch. Retrieved from Onmilwaukee.com website:

https://onmilwaukee.com/articles/interview-with-a-witch

Beyer, C. (n.d.). The difference between magic and magick. Retrieved from Learnreligions.com website: https://www.learnreligions.com/magic-and-magick-95856

The trouble with witchcraft today. (2019, September 9). Retrieved from Bigissuenorth.com website: https://www.bigissuenorth.com/features/2019/09/the-trouble-with-witchcraft-today

Astrology, T. O. I. (2020, December 1). What is Black Magic? How can we protect ourselves from it? Retrieved from Times Of India website:

https://timesofindia.indiatimes.com/religion/rituals-puja/what-is-black-magic-how-can-we-protect-ourselves-from-it/articleshow/79510148.cms

Suggestions for Help. (n.d.). Retrieved from Mit.edu website: https://www.mit.edu/~rei/spir-help.html

Pentagram. (n.d.). Retrieved from Newworldencyclopedia.org website: https://www.newworldencyclopedia.org/entry/Pentagram

Herstik, G. (2018, March 12). Ask A witch: All about candle magick. Retrieved from Nylon.com website: https://www.nylon.com/life/ask-a-witch-candle-magick

Wigington, P. (n.d.). What is sympathetic magic? Retrieved from Learnreligions.com website: https://www.learnreligions.com/sympathetic-magic-2561922

Do you have to ask permission before casting a spell? What if it's for their own good? (n.d.). Retrieved from Quora.com website: https://www.quora.com/Do-you-have-to-ask-permission-before-casting-a-spell-What-if-its-for-their-own-good

Dog, M. (2015, April 30). Magic and White Magic Spells. Learningwitchcraft.Com. https://learningwitchcraft.com/magic-and-white-magic-spells/

Garis, M. G. (2019, October 10). A real witch's 6 tips for using witchcraft to give your home an energy-clearing makeover. Well+Good. https://www.wellandgood.com/how-to-cast-spell-home-energy

Meditation for increasing positive energy: How it works. (n.d.). Artofliving.Org. Retrieved from https://www.artofliving.org/in-en/meditation/meditation-for-you/meditation-for-positive-energy

Mindful Meditations to Boost Your Energy – dummies. (2016, March 26). Dummies.Com. https://www.dummies.com/religion/spirituality/mindful-meditations-to-boost-your-energy

Sponsor. (2020, November 16). Magic spells guide for beginners (9 safety tips to know) – SF weekly. Sfweekly.Com. https://www.sfweekly.com/sponsored/magic-spells-guide-for-beginners-9-safety-tips-to-know

Magick yourself up some happiness and success with these simple spells. (2020, October 14).

Retrieved from Calmmoment.com website:

https://www.calmmoment.com/living/magick-yourself-up-some-happiness-and-success-with-these-simple-spells

Bejelly, K. (2021, May 28). An introduction to magical essential oils. Retrieved from

Agirlworthsaving.net website:https:/agirlworthsaving.net/an-introduction-to-magical-essential-oils

Hines, M. (2020, October 16). Millennial money witch Jessie DaSilva's top tricks, tips, spells.

Forbes Magazine. Retrieved from

https://www.forbes.com/sites/morganhines/2020/10/16/millennial-money-witch-jessie-dasilvas-top-tricks-tips-spells

Lett, D. (2017, September 11). 7 herbs you need in your white witch's apothecary. Retrieved from Soulandspiritmagazine.com website:

https://www.soulandspiritmagazine.com/7-herbs-need-white-witchs-apothecary

Vats, V. D. (2019, September 27). 9 magical herbs for prosperity, protection, and love you should keep at home. Retrieved from India Times website:

https://www.indiatimes.com/lifestyle/magical-herbs-for-success-love-prosperity-376629.html

Rose, B. (2020, June 19). How to charge oils for your magical rituals. Retrieved from Wiccangathering.com website: https://www.wiccangathering.com/how-to-charge-oils-wicca

Clarke, L. (2020, March 22). Wiccan herbs beginners tutorial · Wiccan gathering. Retrieved from Wiccangathering.com website:

https://www.wiccangathering.com/an-introduction-to-wiccan-herbs

Gaiam. (n.d.). How to use visualization to heal physically or emotionally. Retrieved from Gaiam.com website:

https://www.gaiam.com/blogs/discover/how-to-use-visualization-to-heal-physically-or-emotionally

Hines, M. (2020, October 16). Millennial money witch Jessie DaSilva's top tricks, tips, spells. Forbes Magazine. Retrieved from

https://www.forbes.com/sites/morganhines/2020/10/16/millennial-money-witch-jessie-dasilvas-top-tricks-tips-spells

Montell, A. (n.d.). How to cast a happiness spell on yourself, according to a real-life witch. Retrieved from Byrdie.com website: https://www.byrdie.com/spell-for-happiness

The Irish Times. (2018, October 27). Smudge and sweep out negative vibes. Irish Times. Retrieved from

https://www.irishtimes.com/life-and-style/homes-and-property/smudge-and-sweep-out-negative-vibes-1.3675601

teaandrosemary. (2020, October 16). The 10 most powerful & simple healing spells in witchcraft. Retrieved from Teaandrosemary.com website:

https://teaandrosemary.com/healing-spells-in-witchcraft

Basics of magic: Clearing and charging ritual tools – Wicca living. (2017, June 16).

Wiccaliving.Com. https://wiccaliving.com/clearing-charging-ritual-tools

Slick, M., & Wayne, L. (2008, December 9). Sabbats: Sacred festivals of the wiccan reglion. Carm.Org. https://carm.org/wicca/the-wiccan-sabbats-or-holy-days

Wiccan beliefs & common practices. (2015, April 11). Wiccanuniverse.Com. https://www.wiccanuniverse.com/what-is-wicca/beliefspractices

Wiccan Holidays: Celebrating the Sun on the Sabbats – dummies. (2016, March 26). Dummies.Com. https://www.dummies.com/religion/paganism/wiccan-holidays-celebrating-the-sun-on-the-sabbats

Wigington, P. (n.d.-a). A Year of Pagan Sabbat Rituals. Learnreligions.Com. Retrieved from https://www.learnreligions.com/year-of-pagan-sabbat-rituals-2562850

Wigington, P. (n.d.-b). Hold a family Yule Log ritual to celebrate the winter solstice. Learnreligions.Com. Retrieved from https://www.learnreligions.com/family-yule-log-ceremony-2562988

Wigington, P. (n.d.-c). Hold an Imbolc candle ritual for solitary pagans. Learnreligions.Com. Retrieved from https://www.learnreligions.com/hold-an-imbolc-candle-ritual-for-solitaries-2562108

https://www.patheos.com/blogs/witchonfire/2017/04/rites-beltane-sacred-marriage-tying-knot

Witch on Fire. (2018, January 29). Sabbat rituals. Patheos.Com. https://www.patheos.com/blogs/witchonfire/sabbat-rituals

Witch on Fire. (2019, April 19). Beltane sabbat index: Rituals, crafts, and aphrodisiacs for witch's high spring. Patheos.Com. https://www.patheos.com/blogs/witchonfire/2019/04/beltane-sabbat-index-rituals-crafts-and-aphrodisiacs

Faragher, A. K. (2018, March 26). How to cast your own spells at home. Allure. https://www.allure.com/story/how-to-cast-spells

Here are the steps to casting spells that unquestionably work. (n.d.). Semasan.Com. Retrieved from https://www.semasan.com/sema/inc/?here_are_the_steps_to_casting_spells_that_unquestionably_work.html

Mildon, E. (2020, May 8). Don't know your spirit animal? Here's exactly how to find out.

Mindbodygreen.Com; mindbodygreen. https://www.mindbodygreen.com/articles/how-to-find-your-spirit-animal

Richardson, T. C. (2017, February 16). A psychic explains how to find your spiritual guidance squad. Mindbodygreen.Com; mindbodygreen. https://www.mindbodygreen.com/0-28854/a-psychic-explains-how-to-find-your-spiritual-guidance-squad.html

Richardson, T. C. (2018, May 8). How to recognize when the universe gives you A sign (and make it happen more often). Mindbodygreen.Com; mindbodygreen. https://www.mindbodygreen.com/articles/how-to-recognize-when-the-universe-is-giving-you-a-sign

Richardson, T. C. (2021, March 17). 6 types of spirit guides & how to communicate with them. Mindbodygreen.Com; mindbodygreen. https://www.mindbodygreen.com/0-17129/how-to-effectively-communicate-with-your-spirit-guides.html

Wigington, P. (n.d.). 4 types of spirit guides you should know. Learnreligions.Com. from https://www.learnreligions.com/what-is-a-spirit-guide-2561758

Sponsor. (2020, November 16). Magic spells guide for beginners (9 safety tips to know) - SF weekly. Retrieved from Sfweekly.com website: https://www.sfweekly.com/sponsored/magic-spells-guide-for-beginners-9-safety-tips-to-know

Mueller, M., Kovnesky, L., & Snyder, M. (2020, October 26). Hold my broom: Here's real talk from a "real" witch. Retrieved from Onmilwaukee.com website: https://onmilwaukee.com/articles/interview-with-a-witch

www.ingramcontent.com/pod-product-compliance
Lightning Source LLC
Chambersburg PA
CBHW072155200426
43209CB00052B/1269